Early Childhood
Education and Care
in the USA

National Center for
Early Development & Learning

A series from the National Center
for Early Development & Learning

Series Editor: Donald B. Bailey, Jr., Ph.D.

This book is part of a series edited by Donald B. Bailey, Jr., Ph.D., and developed in conjunction with the National Center for Early Development & Learning (NCEDL). Books in this series are designed to serve as resources for sharing new knowledge to enhance the cognitive, social, and emotional development of children from birth through 8 years of age. For information on other books in this series, please refer to the Brookes web site at www.brookespublishing.com.

Other Books in this Series

The Transition to Kindergarten
Robert C. Pianta and Martha J. Cox

Infants and Toddlers in Out-of-Home Care
Debby Cryer and Thelma Harms

Critical Thinking About Critical Periods
Donald B. Bailey, Jr., John T. Bruer,
Frank J. Symons, and Jeff W. Lichtman

Teaching 4- to 8-Year-Olds:
Literacy, Math, Multiculturalism, and Classroom Community
Carollee Howes

Early Childhood Education and Care in the USA

edited by

Debby Cryer, Ph.D.

and

Richard M. Clifford, Ph.D.

Frank Porter Graham Child Development Institute
University of North Carolina at Chapel Hill

National Center for
Early Development & Learning

·P·A·U·L·H·
BROOKES
PUBLISHING CO®

Baltimore • London • Sydney

Paul H. Brookes Publishing Co.
Post Office Box 10624
Baltimore, Maryland 21285-0624

www.brookespublishing.com

Typeset by Auburn Associates, Inc., Baltimore, Maryland.
Manufactured in the United States of America by
Victor Graphics, Inc., Baltimore, Maryland.

The National Center for Early Development & Learning is supported under the
Educational Research and Development Centers Program, PR/Award Number
R307A960004, as administered by the Office of Educational Research and
Improvement, U.S. Department of Education. However, no official endorsement by
the federal government should be inferred.

Library of Congress Cataloging-in-Publication Data
Early childhood education and care in the USA / edited by Debby Cryer and
Richard M. Clifford.
     p.   cm.
  Includes bibliographical references and index.
  ISBN 1-55766-638-5
    1. Early childhood education–Government policy–United States. 2. Child
care–Government policy–United States. I. Cryer, Debby. II. Clifford,
Richard M. III. National Center for Early Development & Learning (U.S.)

LB1139.25.E255 2003
372.21–dc21   2002028233

British Library Cataloguing in Publication data are available from the British Library.

Contents

Contents

About the Editors

Debby Cryer, Ph.D., Scientist, Frank Porter Graham Child Development Institute, University of North Carolina at Chapel Hill, Campus Box 8040, 300 Bank of America Center, Chapel Hill, North Carolina 27599-8040

Dr. Cryer has combined her interests as an early childhood practitioner with those of a researcher, studying real-world issues and translating research findings into practice for early childhood program staff, parents, and policy makers. In addition to studying child care, she has worked on the development of numerous early childhood program quality assessment instruments. With Thelma Harms and Richard Clifford, Dr. Cryer has developed a variety of well-known resources for teachers and for others interested in early childhood education and care (ECEC), including the Infant/Toddler Environment Rating Scale (ITERS; Teachers College Press, 1990) and the Early Childhood Environment Rating Scale–Revised Edition (ECERS-R; Teachers College Press, 1998).

Richard M. Clifford, Ph.D., Senior Scientist, Frank Porter Graham Child Development Institute; Research Associate Professor, School of Education; and Co-director, National Center for Early Development & Learning and the National Prekindergarten Center, University of North Carolina at Chapel Hill, Campus Box 8040, 300 Bank of America Center, Chapel Hill, North Carolina 27599

Dr. Clifford's training is in educational administration with specializations in political science and research. He has taught and has served as a principal in public schools. For more than 25 years, he has studied public policies and advised government officials and practitioners on policies affecting children and families. His work focuses on two major areas: public financing of programs for young children and the provision of appropriate learning environments for preschool and early school-age children. Dr. Clifford is co-author of a widely used series of instruments for evaluating learning environments for children, including the Family Day Care Rating Scale (FDCRS; Teachers College Press, 1989), co-authored with Thelma Harms, and the Infant/Toddler Environment Rating Scale (ITERS; Teachers College Press, 1990) and the Early Childhood Environment Rating Scale–Revised Edition (ECERS-R; Teachers College Press, 1998), both co-authored with Thelma Harms and Debby Cryer. In 1993–1994, Dr. Clifford helped establish and served as the first director of the Division of Child Development in the North Carolina Department of Human Resources and helped with the design and implementation of the state's Smart Start early childhood initiative. He is a past president of the National Association for the Education of Young Children (NAEYC).

About the Contributors

W. Steven Barnett, Ph.D., Professor of Education Economics and Public Policy, and Director, National Institute for Early Education Research, Rutgers University, 120 Albany Street, New Brunswick, New Jersey 08901

Dr. Barnett's work includes research on early education and child care policy, the educational opportunities and experiences of young children in low-income urban areas, the long term effects of preschool programs on children's learning and development, and benefit–cost analysis of preschool programs and their long-term effects. His publications include *Lives in the Balance* (High/Scope Press, 1996), a benefit–cost analysis of preschool education based on a 25-year study, and *Early Care and Education for Children in Poverty* (co-edited with Sarane Spence Boocock; State University of New York Press, 1998).

Barbara T. Bowman, M.Ed., Professor and President, Erikson Institute, 420 North Wabash Avenue, Chicago, Illinois 60611

Ms. Bowman is an authority on early education and a founder and currently president of the Erikson Institute. She has taught at the preschool and primary levels and in colleges and universities. She is a frequent speaker at conferences and universities in the United States and abroad. Her specialty areas are early education, cultural diversity, and education of children at risk. In addition to teaching, Ms. Bowman has directed a wide range of projects and served on numerous professional boards.

Moncrieff Cochran, Ph.D., Professor, Department of Human Development, and Director, Cornell Early Childhood Program,

College of Human Ecology, Cornell University, G35 Martha Van Rensselaer Hall, Ithaca, New York 14853

Dr. Cochran's research and program development work have focused on contexts for early development: early childhood education and care (ECEC), home–school relations, the social networks of parents and children, and the parent empowerment process. Editor of the *International Handbook of Child Care Policies and Programs* (Greenwood Press, 1993), he more recently co-authored *Child Care that Works: A Parent's Guide to Finding Quality Child Care* with Eva Cochran (Robins Lane Press, 2000). Dr. Cochran is currently writing a book that applies lessons learned from his international child care research program to the U.S. child care scene. He recently completed a term on the governing board of the National Association for the Education of Young Children (NAEYC).

Victoria R. Fu, Ph.D., Professor of Child Development, Department of Human Development, Virginia Polytechnic Institute and State University, Blacksburg, Virginia 24061

Dr. Fu's research focuses on contextual influences on how people learn; on inquiry-based, social constructivist approaches to teaching and learning; and on the process of transformation in teacher education. She has published extensively in professional journals and books, including *Affirming Diversity Through Democratic Conversations* (co-edited with Andrew Stremmel; Prentice Hall, 1999) and *Teaching and Learning: Collaborative Exploration of the Reggio Emilia Approach* (co-edited with Andrew Stremmel and Lynn T. Hall; Prentice Hall, 2002).

Shirley Gatenio, Ph.D., Manager, Clearinghouse for International Developments in Child, Youth and Family Policies, Columbia University, 622 West 113th Street, McVickar, Mail Code 4600, New York, New York, 10025

Dr. Gatenio has directed public policy analyses, lobbying, and community organization efforts for governmental and voluntary organizations and is an adjunct lecturer at the Columbia University School of Social Work. Her areas of interest are family and child policy and policy implementation.

Sharon Lynn Kagan, Ed.D., Professor of Early Childhood and Family Policy, Co-director, National Center for Children and Families, Teachers College, Columbia University, 525 West 120th Street, Box 226, New York, New York 10027

Dr. Kagan is the Virginia and Leonard Marx Professor of Early Childhood and Family Policy at Teachers College, Columbia University, and a Professor Adjunct at Yale University's Child Study Center. Author of more than 100 articles and 12 books, Dr. Kagan focuses her research on the institutions and policies that affect child and family life. Dr. Kagan consults with numerous federal and state agencies, Congress, governors, and legislators; is a member of 40 national boards; and is a past president of the National Association for the Education of Young Children (NAEYC) and of Family Support America, a non-profit organization committed to advancing the well-being of families and the family support programs that serve them.

Sheila B. Kamerman, D.S.W., Professor; Co-director, Clearinghouse for International Developments in Child, Youth and Family Policies; and Director, Institute for Child and Family Policy, Columbia University School of Social Work, 622 West 113th Street, McVickar, Mail Code 4600, New York, New York, 10025

Dr. Kamerman is the Compton Foundation Centennial Professor for the Prevention of Children and Youth Problems at the Columbia University School of Social Work; Director of The Institute for Child and Family Policy at Columbia University, a university-wide institute established in 1999; and Co-director of the Cross-National Studies Research Program. Her current research activities include a 20-country study of family change and family policies since World War II, a study of "best practices" in contracting for child and family social services, and several studies on early childhood education and care (ECEC). Dr. Kamerman has published extensively and consulted widely.

Naomi Karp, M.Ed., Director, National Institute on Early Childhood Development and Education, Office of Educational Research and Improvement, U.S. Department of Education, 555 New Jersey Avenue, NW, Room 606d, Washington, D.C. 20208

Naomi Karp served as the coordinator for the U.S. portion of the study of early education and care policies conducted by the Organisation for Economic Co-operation and Development (OECD).

Lilian G. Katz, Ph.D., Director, ERIC Clearinghouse on Elementary and Early Childhood Education, and Professor Emerita of Early Childhood Education, College of Education, University of Illinois, Urbana-Champaign, 805 West Pennsylvania Avenue, Urbana, Illinois 61081

Dr. Katz is Professor Emerita of Early Childhood Education at the University of Illinois, Urbana-Champaign, where she is also Director of the ERIC Clearinghouse on Elementary and Early Childhood Education. She has authored many publications about early childhood education, teacher education, child development, and parenting. Dr. Katz is also Editor of the first on-line early childhood journal, *Early Childhood Research & Practice,* and is a past president of the National Association for the Education of Young Children (NAEYC).

Leonard N. Masse, Ed.D., Research Fellow, National Institute for Early Education Research, Rutgers University, 120 Albany Street, New Brunswick, New Jersey 08901

Dr. Masse is a public school mathematics teacher and a research fellow at the National Institute for Early Education Research at Rutgers University. He completed his doctorate in education from Rutgers University in 2002. His work includes research on child care funding and policy, benefit–cost analysis of preschool programs, and teaching mathematics. Recent publications include "A Benefit–Cost Analysis of the Abecedarian Early Childhood Intervention" (co-authored with W. Steven Barnett; *American Education Finance Association 2002 Yearbook*) and "The Possibility of Perfection" (*Math Teaching in the Middle School,* May 2001).

Kristin Moore, Ph.D., President and Senior Scholar, Child Trends, 4301 Connecticut Avenue, NW, Washington, D.C. 20008

Dr. Moore is a social psychologist and President and Senior Scholar of Child Trends, a nonprofit, nonpartisan research organization that focuses on children and families. She has been with Child Trends since 1982, studying trends in child and family well-being, the effects of family structure and social change on children, positive development, the determinants and consequences of adolescent parenthood, and the effects of welfare and welfare reform on children. She is a member of the Family and Child Well-being Research Network, which was established by the National Institute of Child Health and Human Development (NICHD) to examine the factors that enhance the development and well-being of children. In addition, Dr. Moore serves on the Advisory Council for NICHD. In 1999, she received the Foundation for Child Development Centennial Award for linking research on children's development to policies that serve the public interest. In 2002 she was selected to be Visiting Scholar by the Society for Adolescent Medicine.

Gwen G. Morgan, Founding Director, Wheelock College Institute for Leadership and Career Initiatives, Wheelock College, 200 The Riverway, Boston, Massachusetts 02215

Gwen G. Morgan has been in the early childhood education and care (ECEC) field since roughly 1965 and has written extensively and received numerous awards. She now teaches at Wheelock College and is Founding Director of the Wheelock College Institute for Leadership and Career Initiatives. The institute maintains current data comparing state child care licensing rules and policies and provides research and technical assistance on professional development in ECEC. Gwen G. Morgan has written widely on policy issues in this field.

Edna Runnels Ranck, Ed.D., Consultant in Early Care and Education, Washington, D.C.

Dr. Ranck has directed early childhood programs, taught in higher education, and served in various policy-related capacities in the New

Jersey Department of Human Services. She was director of public policy and research for the National Association of Child Care Resource and Referral Agencies (NACCRRA) from 1998 to 2002. She has published articles, newsletter columns, and book chapters and has presented papers and workshops at national and international conferences. Dr. Ranck, a member of Phi Beta Kappa, is listed in *Who's Who in America* and *Who's Who in the World*.

Jerry West, Ph.D., Program Director, Early Childhood and Household Studies Program, National Center for Education Statistics, 1990 K Street, NW, Room 9042, Washington, D.C. 20006

Dr. West received his doctorate in sociology from the University of North Carolina at Chapel Hill. He joined the National Center for Education Statistics (NCES) in 1987 after working as a research director in the private sector. He is presently director of the Early Childhood Household Studies Program at NCES. Dr. West has authored many NCES publications in the areas of father involvement, child care and early childhood education, school readiness, and kindergarten in the United States.

Introduction

Naomi Karp

If we fail the children, we all fail.
—*Pearl S. Buck*

BACKGROUND

In 1998, the United States agreed to participate in a 12-nation study of early childhood education and care (ECEC) policies, an effort undertaken by the Organisation for Economic Co-operation and Development (OECD). The OECD evolved from the Marshall Plan at the end of World War II. Over the years OECD has shifted its focus from rebuilding war-torn Europe to one of strengthening the economies of all of its 29 industrialized member nations. The OECD also is helping to build market economies in developing countries. In addition, the OECD is studying how social policies affect economic markets.

Perhaps one of the best examples of the interplay between the economic and labor markets and social policies is in the area of ECEC policies. The provision of care and education for young children is a necessary condition for ensuring equal access for women to the labor market. Moreover, research continues to document that high-quality education and care are the foundations for lifelong learning and development.

If nations are to have strong economies and full employment, then ECEC policies need to ensure that working mothers can be secure in knowing that their children will be in optimal care giving environments. In reality, however, access to high-quality ECEC programs is not equitable, resulting in many children arriving at school not ready to succeed. This also causes problems for many mothers because although they need additional income, they do not want to leave their children in poor-quality environments.

Therefore, in 1998, for the first time in 20 years, the OECD began a comparative international thematic review of ECEC policies. The study examined policies, programs, and services for children from birth through 8 years of age and their families. The countries taking part in the study from the fall of 1998 through the spring of 2000 included Australia, Belgium, the Czech Republic, Denmark, Finland, Italy, the Netherlands, Norway, Portugal, Sweden, Switzerland, and the United States. The U.S. portion of the study took place from September 26, 1999, through October 8, 1999.

The U.S. Department of Education coordinated the U.S. portion of the thematic review. The U.S. Department of Health and Human Services provided financial support for review activities carried out in the United States. The federal agencies supporting this study believe that improving quality, access, and equity in ECEC policies is of paramount importance. A study comparing the United States' ECEC policies with those of 11 other industrialized countries seemed like a perfect vehicle for calling attention to our strengths and our shortcomings.

CONCEPTION AND DESIGN OF THE STUDY

Before the study began, the OECD convened small meetings of early childhood experts who developed a common framework of topics and questions to be addressed in each country. The OECD established a precise process for conducting the reviews across the participating countries.

The agreed-on purpose of the review was to provide cross-national information needed to improve ECEC policies in all OECD member countries. Specifically, the review tried to accomplish the following:

1. Distinguish among and investigate the contexts, major policy concerns, and policy responses to address the concerns within the participating countries.

2. Explore the roles of national government, nongovernmental organizations, and other partners and the institutional resources devoted to planning and implementing services at each level.

3. Identify feasible policy options suited to the different contexts.

4. Evaluate the impact, coherence, and effectiveness of different approaches ECEC policy and practice.

5. Highlight particularly innovative policies and practices.

6. Contribute to the Indicators of Education Systems project by identifying the types of data and instruments that need to be developed in support of ECEC information collection, policy making, research, monitoring, and evaluation.

A team of site reviewers, selected by OECD, visited each participating country for approximately 10 days. The reviewers were from OECD member nations, but they did not live in the country under review. The roles of families, communities, and other environmental influences on children's early learning and development were of great importance in the review process. Of particular interest were issues related to access to services, the quality of the services, and equity.

The OECD selected the following people to serve as the U.S. site visit team, with Michelle Neuman as the U.S. site coordinator:

1. Patrizia Ghedini, from Italy (Ms. Ghedini was unable to complete the review)

2. Jytte Juul Jensen, from Denmark, Director of the Danish Early Childhood Paraprofessional Training Program

3. Pamela Oberhuemer, from Germany, Research Office in the German Education Department

4. Mark Weekenborg, from the Netherlands, Ministry of Education

The reviewers placed a great deal of emphasis on learning how policies are developed in the following areas:

1. Regulations

2. Staffing

3. Pedagogy and curriculum

4. Family engagement and support

5. Funding and financing

The OECD also determined how the site visits would be conducted in each country. Children were observed in different types of education and child care environments. The review team visited about 35 different types of early childhood programs in fewer than 10 days. The places included family child care homes, a lab school on a university campus, public school pre-kindergarten classes, for-profit and not-for-profit child care centers, and faith-based child care programs. In addition, the observation teams met with officials from local, state, and federal governments. They also met with families of young children, advocates, researchers, and administrators of different types of programs.

In addition to a team of site reviewers visiting each participating country, a large part of the OECD review process involved the preparation of papers and reports. The study coordinators in the participating countries and the visitors were responsible, at different times, for producing the following documents according to OECD standards:

1. *Background Report:* A Background Report was written by experts within each country and given to the site review team prior to their arrival in the country to be reviewed. The Background Reports are based on a common framework of detailed questions. This book is based on the papers contained in the report for the United States.

2. *Country Note:* Following each participating nation's site visit, the OECD Secretariat prepared a Country Note. The information in this document contains references from the Background Report; the review team's observations and assessments; and data obtained in discussions with officials, educators, researchers, and others with whom the review team met during the visit. The Country Note provides insights into current practices and policies. In addition, it describes major challenges facing the country, how national goals are met, and makes recommendations for policy options designed to improve and ensure quality, access, and equity. The U.S. Country Note is available on the web site for the

National Institute on Early Childhood Development and Education, which is within the U.S. Department of Education (go to http://www.ed.gov/offices/OERI/ECI/hottopics.html and click on "Country Note").

3. *Comparative Report:* This document was completed by OECD at the conclusion of the 12-nation study. It contains a comparative review and analysis of the ECEC policies in the participating nations. The comparative report was published in 2001 by the OECD as *Starting Strong: Early Childhood Education and Care* (available from Paul H. Brookes Publishing Co.).

ROLE OF THE UNITED STATES IN THE STUDY

In the spring of 1999, before the U.S. site visit, a small group of early childhood researchers who had extensive international experience convened to serve as a steering committee for the U.S. portion of the study. Richard M. Clifford, Moncrieff Cochran, Victoria R. Fu, Sharon Lynn Kagan, and Sheila B. Kamerman served in this capacity and developed criteria for selecting states to visit. On the basis of geographic considerations, status of early childhood services, size of the state, population and diversity, and other factors, the steering committee recommended visiting Colorado, North Carolina, and Ohio.

The steering committee also recommended authors for the Background Report. This report would be a critical piece of information for the reviewers, explaining the "nuts and bolts" of ECEC policies in the United States. Thus, the authors, who are also the authors of the chapters in this book, were selected because they have a thorough grasp of the contexts, major issues and concerns, distinctive policies, creative approaches to service provision, and available program evaluation data regarding U.S. early childhood service provision. The papers these authors wrote for the U.S. Background Report addressed the context of ECEC in the United States, quality of services, access, regulatory policy, staffing, program content (curriculum) and implementation (pedagogy), family engagement and support, funding issues, evaluation and research, and concluding comments/assessments.

WHAT WE LEARNED

As a result of taking part in the thematic review, the United States has a body of knowledge that will advance the field of ECEC. The time, effort, and thought that the authors put into the chapters in this book provide current data and findings in key early childhood policy areas.

Hopefully, every community concerned about the future of our youngest and most vulnerable citizens will reflect on and seriously discuss the documentation provided in this book and in the Country Note prepared by the OECD Secretariat. Then, each community can work to ensure that early childhood environments are truly high-quality learning environments. The Country Note contains critical and wise input from the OECD visitors to the United States. It offers some recommendations for action, action aimed at improving the development and learning of all young children in the United States.

The quality found by the review team ranged from extremely high to extremely low. Quality, access, and equity appeared to be income based across the states. Many children are thriving. Many are not. The achievement gap is beginning long before many children ever reach the front door of an elementary school.

The Comparative Report, *Starting Strong: Early Childhood Education and Care*, was released by the OECD in June 2001. It gives us a picture of how the United States compares with 11 other industrialized nations on specific dimensions of ECEC policies. This report should also give us the incentive to make a commitment that all young children in the United States will have access to high-quality ECEC.

ACKNOWLEDGMENTS

The United States would not have been able to participate in the OECD's study of early childhood education and care (ECEC) had it not been for the hard work and dedication of many people in the United States and across the Atlantic Ocean. Special recognition and thanks go to the following people.

The authors of the papers that compose the Background Report and the chapters in this book are to be commended for their heroic efforts. Not only did each author produce high-quality work, but the initial draft was completed in approximately 1 month. Without these authors, this book would not exist, and the U.S. site visit would not have taken place.

Debby Cryer has made this publication possible. Her superb editorial skills, patience with federal rules, and general knowledge of the field are greatly appreciated, as is her good nature.

Michelle Neuman, the coordinator of the entire early childhood thematic review in the United States, has done a phenomenal job of carrying out this effort. Organizational, technical, and writing skills as excellent as Michelle's are rare. Her understanding of policy is outstanding. Her contributions will have a major, long-lasting impact on the field.

The OECD review team was a remarkable group of people. The 10-day trip to three states was enjoyable and educational because of the team members' unbounded energy and stamina, their keen intellect and sense of humor, and their incredible command of the English language. Daily they were subjected to huge numbers of acronyms, confusing provisions in legislation, and multiple names of state programs, but they never flinched. The U.S. Country Note reflects the team's dedication. The early childhood community owes them a debt of gratitude.

The coordinators in each state performed their jobs with great speed and precision, also on very short notice. The meetings with community leaders, educators, and families and the observations of children were excellent and gave the review team a good picture of how confusing our early childhood "system" can be.

Coordinators were selected in each state to make sure hotel rooms, vans, classrooms, meetings, meals, and other details were in place. Richard M. Clifford was responsible for making arrangements in North Carolina, the late Mary L. Culkin arranged visits and meetings in Colorado, and Jane Wiechel coordinated activities in Ohio.

In addition, Richard M. Clifford made it possible for everyone who needed to be paid to get their money. He also took care of too many details to count. His in-kind contributions of time and other resources to this effort are truly appreciated.

Wanda Weaver of the National Center for Early Development & Learning (NCEDL) made sure that everyone who needed a ticket to get some place had the papers needed to get there. She also made sure that food, meeting rooms, hotels, and other necessities were available. She smiled throughout the process.

Last, but by no means least, we all pulled so hard to make sure that this study was successful because of the young children of Colorado, North Carolina, and Ohio and the rest of our nation. We want them to have the best experiences, opportunities, and environments possible so that they will be successful in school and beyond.

Early Childhood Education and Care in the USA

National Center for
Early Development & Learning

1

Overview of the Current Policy Context

Sheila B. Kamerman and Shirley Gatenio

Early childhood education and care (ECEC) in the United States includes a wide range of part-day, full school-day, and full work-day programs under educational, social welfare, and commercial auspices. These programs are funded and delivered in a variety of ways in both the public and the private sectors and are designed sometimes with an emphasis on the care component of ECEC and at other times with stress on education or with equal attention to both.

DEFINITIONS

Early Childhood Education and Care Programs

The *ECEC programs* discussed in this chapter include preschools (pre-kindergartens, compensatory education programs, and nursery schools operated under education auspices), kindergartens, center-based child care (often defined as programs in nonresidential settings that provide education and/or care to children and that include organized group programs such as Head Start), and family child care (both regulated and unregulated child minding). Parental care, relative care, occasional babysitting, and care provided in a child's own home are not included in this chapter nor are programs only for children with special needs.

Preschools include the range of programs offered under public and private education auspices or providing compensatory education under special legislation, usually serve children from age 2–3 to compulsory school entry, are largely half-day or cover the normal school day (usually about 6 hours, e.g., 9:00 A.M. to 3:00 P.M.), and cover the normal school year.

Center-based child care typically refers to full-day programs under social welfare auspices (e.g., Head Start) or free-standing and independent programs that offer care corresponding to the traditional working hours (e.g., 9:00 A.M. to 5:00 P.M., 7:00 A.M. to 6:00 P.M.) and are open 5 days a week for the full year. Although most centers provide care to children ages 3–5 years, some provide care for infants and toddlers (1–2 years of age) as well. At their discretion, some child care centers also may care for school-age children in their after-school programs. There is substantial variation in the ages of children for whom care is offered. Almost all centers are regulated or licensed in some way by the states with regard to health and safety standards, staff–child ratios, maximum number of children per group, and nutrition and have, at the least, annual inspections.

Family child care refers to care for several children (other than the provider's own) in the provider's own home. States regulate family child care homes through licensing or registration regarding one or more of the following criteria: square footage for activities, staff–child ratios, preservice training requirements, criminal backgrounds, and immunization requirements. Licensing typically requires providers to meet minimum health, nutrition, and safety standards; to limit the number of children in a home; and to sometimes conform to programmatic standards. Registration, by comparison, requires or encourages providers to self-identify themselves to the state and certify that they comply with state requirements. Registration typically involves fewer inspections than licensing. In 1993, only eight states and the District of Columbia required that family child care providers be registered or licensed (Ewen, Blank, Hart, & Schulman, 2002). Family child care may occur during standard hours or during irregular hours (e.g., nights, weekends). The upper limit is 6 children in family child care homes. Group family child care homes are private homes that provide care for sometimes as many as 12 children. These group family child care homes are often required to employ at least one other adult to assist in the care of the children and are more likely to be licensed than family child care homes. The number of hours and days of care provided is negotiated between the parent and provider in these home-based settings but are generally available to accommodate the needs of parents working full time throughout the year. Some states specify the maximum number of infants and toddlers that a provider can care for in his or her home; the maximum varies with the age of the child.

Policies

ECEC *policies* include the whole range of government actions (federal, state, and sometimes local) that influence the supply and/or demand for ECEC and program quality. These government activities include the following:

- Direct delivery of ECEC services, such as public school–based kindergartens and prekindergarten programs
- Direct and indirect financial subsidies to private providers of education and care, such as grants, contracts, and tax incentives
- Financial subsidies to parents/consumers of ECEC, such as grants and tax benefits to permit or facilitate access to services or to permit parents to remain at home and withdraw for a brief period from the labor force at the time of childbirth or adoption
- Establishment and enforcement of regulations, such as those pertaining to staff–children ratio and health and safety

Generally, ECEC policies cover children from birth through state-designated compulsory school age. Compulsory school age is determined by the individual state and ranges from age 5–8 years (see Table 1.1). Elementary (primary) school is compulsory for all children, but it is at the state's discretion whether kindergarten (the year before primary school begins) enrollment is mandated. Twelve states and the District of Columbia require children to attend kindergarten (Education Commission of the States, 2001/2002). The other 38 states mandate that local school districts provide kindergarten, but it is the parents' decision whether to enroll their child. Parents also have the option of enrolling their children in privately sponsored kindergartens.

Table 1.1. Compulsory school attendance age across the United States (including the District of Columbia)

Compulsory school attendance age	Number of states
Age 5 years	7
Age 6 years	20
Age 7 years	22
Age 8 years	2

Source: Data collected by the Public Affairs Division of the National Association for the Education of Young Children in the spring of 1995.

The primary responsibility for education is at the level of the states. Many state legislatures are taking a leading role in the development of ECEC policies, making larger investments in preschool programs and in programs that respond to the work responsibilities of low-income families, especially those who are dependent on welfare or are at risk of becoming dependent.

There is no debate regarding whether compulsory school age should be changed or even made fully consistent nationally. There is debate, however, with regard to expansion of prekindergarten services and/or the length of the prekindergarten and kindergarten days and which level of government should have responsibility for regulating and setting program standards (Schulman, Blank, & Ewen, 1999).

For most children in ECEC programs, entry into a formal early childhood program begins when the children are between 3 and 5 years old. Because of growing evidence that early intervention can be effective in compensating for early deprivation, mitigating and preventing disabilities in the future, and preparing young children for subsequent schooling (Barnett, 1995; Shonkoff & Phillips, 2000)—and because more women with children younger than 3 years are entering the workforce (Bowman, Donovan, & Burns, 2001)—increased resources have been dedicated to providing services to children younger than 3 years. In addition to care and education, these services may include health and nutritional screenings and may be coupled with family support services for parents, including parent education, nutrition classes, various social service supports, and job training. Specialized programs also work with at-risk individuals, such as pregnant teenagers or substance abusers, even prior to the birth of the child in preparation for parenting. Programs whose primary objective is to support the work efforts of parents accept children from 3 months of age (when federally mandated postchildbirth parental or family leave ends) through school age.

HISTORICAL ROOTS

As in most other advanced industrialized countries, ECEC programs in the United States have evolved out of diverse historical streams, including child protection, early childhood education services for children with special needs, and services to facilitate mothers' labor force participation. The history of ECEC in the United States begins with two developments: 1) day nurseries (child care centers), first established in the 1830s under voluntary auspices and designed to care for the "unfortunate" children of working mothers, and 2) nursery schools, developing from the early education programs in Massachusetts also first established in the 1830s, and the later "kindergarten" programs based on the work of Froebel. The first day nursery was established in 1838 in Boston to care for the children of seamen's wives and widows. Day nurseries expanded subsequently in response to pressures created by the rapid industrialization and massive immigration that took place in the latter part of the century. These nurseries were custodial in nature, focusing primarily on basic care and supervision of the children. By the end of the century, a National Federation of Day Nurseries had been established. During war times—the Civil War, World War I, and World War II—these programs increased in numbers, only to decline when war ended. Kindergartens and nursery schools expanded slowly during the 19th century and experienced a significant increase only during the 1920s, as a form of enriched experience for middle-class children.

Little public support developed in the country for either program type until the mid-1960s and early 1970s, when a confluence of factors led to the significant expansion of both program types. The numbers of ECEC programs—both day care centers and nursery schools—increased dramatically. This expansion both reflected and contributed to a resurgence of national interest in early child development. The War on Poverty included attention to deprived and disadvantaged children and, as a response, the development of compensatory education programs. Researchers stressed the importance of early education as a strategy for both better preparation for school and for ensuring access to health care and improved nutrition. Head Start was established first as a summer program and then as a year-round program. The increase in labor force participation rates by middle-income women raised the issue of the need for quality out-of-home care for children generally. The rising welfare caseload stimulated interest in providing federal funds for child care for women receiving social assistance, for those who had received aid earlier, and for those who were viewed as at risk of needing social assistance. And middle-income parents, regardless of their employment status, increasingly viewed preschool as a valuable experience for their children and essential for facilitating an easier transition to school.

In 1971, Congress enacted the first national child care legislation, but President Nixon vetoed it on the grounds that such a program would constitute an effort at communalizing child rearing. Conservatives mounted a massive campaign throughout the 1970s to block federal child care initiatives and only in the early 1980s began to acknowledge the need for such services, albeit under private auspices. In subsequent years, these diverse initiatives have continued to expand: care for children from low-income families and/or neglected children, care for the children of working parents, compensatory education, and early education to enhance the development of young children. Although ECEC scholars and advocates are increasingly convinced of the need to integrate these program types, categorical funding coupled with diverse societal values continue to support the differences. The result is a fragmented ECEC system, of wide-ranging quality and with skewed access, but with some movement since the late 1990s toward the integration of education and care.

CURRENT POLICY CONTEXT

The United States has no national child and/or family policy, nor does it have a coherent national ECEC policy. Labor market policy, public (social) assistance policy, education policy, and child welfare policy all have had and still have a role in the development of ECEC. The hoped-for outcomes of ECEC, as stated by various proponents, now include the following: increasing the productivity of the current and future workforce; preventing and reducing social problems such as welfare dependency, juvenile delinquency, teenage pregnancy, and school failure; supporting the work efforts of parents on welfare and low-income parents to help them achieve economic self-sufficiency; enhancing the development of young children; and helping parents fulfill their roles as nurturers and teachers for their children by providing skill training (Smith, Fairchild, & Groginsky, 1995).

Changes in the Labor Force

The increased interest in ECEC, dating from the 1960s, results from the convergence of several trends. Chief among them is the dramatic rise in the labor force participation of women, especially married mothers. Beginning in 1975, the labor force participation rate of women with children has exceeded that of women with no children. More striking, in 1960, one fifth of mothers with children younger than 6 years were in the labor force, and the rate more than tripled to 62.3% by 1996. Since the 1980s, the continued increase in labor force participation rates of women with children younger than 6 years, in particular the rise among women with children younger than 3 years, has stimulated the interest in and need for an expanded ECEC system. In 1975, about one third of mothers with children younger than 3 years were employed, compared with nearly 60% of these mothers in 1996. The trends are even more dramatic for mothers of infants younger than 1 year old. An increase in dual-earner families has contributed significantly to the demand for early care and education. In 1996, both parents were employed in 58.6% of families with children younger than 6 years in comparison with 52.6% just a decade earlier (U.S. House of Representatives [USHR], Committee on Ways and Means, 1998).

The rise in the number of lone-mother households has added to the demand, especially for full-day programs, because lone mothers are more likely than married mothers to work full time and because families headed by a lone mother have been a rapidly growing family type. From 1970 to 1996, the number of two-parent families with chil-

Table 1.2. Labor force participation rates (%) of women with children younger than age 6 years by age of youngest child

Year	Total for mothers with youngest child younger than age 6	Total for mothers with youngest child younger than age 3	With youngest child age 2	With youngest child age 1	With youngest child younger than age 1
1960	20.2	—	—	—	—
1975	38.8	34.1	31.5	—	—
1985	53.5	49.5	48.0	—	—
1995	62.3	58.9	64.3	58.0	55.0
2000	64.6	60.4	64.5	62.7	54.6
2001	64.3	60.2	65.8	60.4	54.9

Source: Bureau of Labor Statistics (2002b).

dren increased by 20%, whereas the number of families headed by a lone mother with children rose by 127%, to 12.5 million (USHR, 1998).

The age of the youngest child and the mothers' marital status affect the labor force participation rates of mothers (see Tables 1.2 and 1.3) and are more important factors than the number of children in the family. Divorced mothers have the highest participation rates across all age categories, followed in descending order by married, separated, and widowed mothers. In each of these marital status categories, the labor force participation rate increases as the children grow older.

Whether mothers work full or part time also has consequences for the demand for ECEC. Although about 60% of mothers with children younger than 6 years worked in the late 1990s, about 20% of those did not work full time (at least 35 hours per week). Mothers are more likely to work full time once their youngest child enters school. Divorced mothers are the most likely to work full time, whereas never-married women are the least likely, regardless of the ages of their children.

Welfare Reform

Another major factor that has shaped ECEC policies is the so-called welfare reform legislation of the late 1990s and the provisions of the new public assistance legislation for low-income lone mothers and children. The Personal Responsibility and Work Opportunity Reconciliation Act (PRWORA) of 1996 (PL 104-193), the major wel-

Table 1.3. Labor force participation rates (%) of women with children younger than age 6 years by age of youngest child and marital status, March 2001

	Age of youngest child		
Marital status	Younger than age 6	Between ages 3 and 5	Younger than age 3
Married, spouse present	60.3	64.8	57.3
Divorced	74.1	79.5	66.1
Separated	66.1	74.8	58.2
Widowed	67.3	72.3	60.3
Never married	60.2	71.8	54.1

Source: Bureau of Labor Statistics (2002a).

fare reform initiative of the 1990s, requires that low-income women with children ages 3 months and older engage in work within 2 years of claiming assistance and limits lifetime receipt of assistance to a maximum of 5 years. These requirements mean that by far most low-income lone mothers are now expected to work even when they have infants. One result has been increased Congressional recognition of the need for child care services, even if quality attributes and early education curricula have not received comparable attention.

PRWORA made dramatic changes in child care policy. It consolidated four separate child care funding streams, including the Child Care and Development Block Grant (CCDBG), into a single Child Care and Development Fund (CCDF) and increased the amount of federal money to states for child care both by increasing funding for the child care block grant and by allowing states to transfer funds from PRWORA's Temporary Assistance for Needy Families block grant into child care. (A block grant is a sum of money provided by the federal government to the states to be used at the states' discretion within a broad and flexible framework.) PRWORA also gave states the responsibility for providing child care but ended the earlier entitlement to time-limited ECEC subsidies for assistance-related services. Several states have also increased their subsidies for ECEC in this context.

Despite increases in funding and services, research suggests that large portions of eligible, low-income families are still not getting help (Adams & Rohacek, 2002). Nor is quality a central focus of welfare-related child care policies.

Roles of Federal and State
Governments and the Public Sector

Important in shaping current ECEC policies is the historical division of responsibility between federal and state/local government and the strong emphasis and preference in the society for minimalist government, in particular the rejection of a strong national (federal) role in social—or child and family—policy, and the preference for voluntary (nonprofit) and market (for-profit) sector service provision.

The federal government, through Congress, plays an important role in formulating ECEC polices and goals and facilitates the states' and localities' major roles in the actual implementation of programs to suit the particular needs and preferences of their regions. The federal government's policy-making efforts have primarily focused on making services available to children who are at risk due to economic, biological, social, or psychological circumstances or combinations of these or on providing child care services as an incentive for mothers receiving social assistance to gain entry to the labor force. In addition, the federal government has created opportunities and options for parents through the federal income tax credit for child and dependent care. At the state level, policy decisions are made with regard to eligibility; extent of the supply and availability of services; allocation of services and benefits; and scope and quality of services, including health and safety standards. The states use legislation, supplemental funding, and regulation to implement policy decisions. Since the 1990s, states have also taken the leadership role in developing and implementing prekindergarten services and early intervention services for young children at risk. The allocation of resources and policies varies greatly across and within the states. Some states encourage local government and community participation in the development of early childhood policies through the formation of localized planning groups, funding matches, and the development of local plans as a criterion for state funding. Other states assume near complete fiscal, regulatory, and policy-making responsibilities for ECEC.

As with most social services in the United States, the private sectors (both nonprofit and for-profit) play a major role in ECEC. For example, of all 5-year-olds enrolled in kindergarten in 1996,

84.8% attended public kindergarten programs and 15.2% attended private programs. About half of the children in nursery schools are in private schools. More important, among child care centers in 1990, private providers dominated the delivery system: About 10% were public providers and of the others, about two thirds were nonprofit agencies and one third profit-making businesses. Among the nonprofit centers, 25% were independent nonprofits, 15% were sponsored by a religious organization, 8% were sponsored by larger nonprofits; 8% were sponsored by public schools; and 9% were Head Start providers. About 6% of all for-profit centers were part of child care chains, and 29% were independent (Willer et al., 1991). Family child care is almost all private.

Some employers, usually large firms, have become involved in ECEC typically by providing links with ECEC information and referral services and to a lesser extent by becoming a provider of services to their employees. Such firms may offer employee subsidies or other benefits for child care, such as providing financial support to early childhood centers in the community and participating in local or state collaborations to plan for future early childhood needs.

Government efforts are often monitored by not-for-profit entities that act on behalf of children and families. Some entities are sophisticated institutions that engage in research or advocacy activities or both on a national, state, local, or community level. Other not-for-profit entities may be providers of services that sometimes become active advocates of early childhood policies in their regions, whereas other entities may be more generalized community-based organizations interested in enriching the quality of life in their communities. Charitable foundations are important players in the policy-making arena through their funding of research and innovative programming.

Research on Early Childhood Development and Learning

Research and new knowledge play roles in the development of ECEC policy as well. Research demonstrates the importance of ECEC from birth to school entry in determining the cognitive, social, and emotional well-being of individuals; the earliest years are "believed to offer perhaps singular opportunities for intervention and prevention efforts" (Brooks-Gunn, 1997, p. 2). A comprehensive study carried out by the Carnegie Corporation of New York reviewed research on early child-hood needs and programs and concluded, "How individuals function from preschool years all the way through adolescence and even adult-hood hinges, to a significant extent, on their experiences before the age of three" (Carnegie Corporation of New York, 1994); similar findings are contained in the body of research reviewed in *From Neurons to Neighborhoods: The Science of Early Childhood Development* (Shonkoff & Phillips, 2000).

Growing interest in "readiness" for primary school is still another factor that has generated interest in ECEC in recent years. Research demonstrates that early learning experiences are linked with later school achievement, emotional and social well-being, fewer grade retentions, and reduced incidences of juvenile delinquency and that these outcomes are all factors associated with later adult productivity. Such findings (Barnett, 1995; Berrueta-Clement, Schweinhart, Barnett, Epstein, & Weikart, 1984; Lazar, Darlington, Murray, Royce, & Snipper, 1983; Yoshikawa, 1995) suggest the value of increased investment in ECEC. From this perspective, ECEC is increasingly viewed as a cost-efficient and cost-effective strategy whose benefits are reaped both during the school careers of each child and in the future economy. As the demand for competent and highly skilled workers increases while the numbers of younger workers is projected to decrease, it is critical that the potential of each member of society be realized. ECEC is appreciated as helping to provide future workers with a solid foundation of skills, competencies, and attitudes that enhances their opportunities to develop the skills needed to success-fully compete in the increasingly competitive economy.

Knowledge–Policy Discrepancy

In short, multiple policy and program factors have contributed to the development of a fragmented ECEC delivery system that is clearly not yet fully responsive to the dramatic social and demographic changes that have occurred, in particular the rise in labor force par-ticipation of women with young children and the increased proportion of children reared in lone mother families. Moreover, the United States is world renowned for its extensive and rigorous child development research. In this context it is even more surprising how extensive a gap there is between the state of knowledge regarding child development and child well-being on the one hand and the public policy response as reflected in national ECEC policies on the other.

American society has long been conflicted in its attitude toward women and their roles and in its attitude toward government and the family and their appropriate roles. This tension emerges repeatedly in discussions regarding ECEC policies. Low-income lone mothers are expected to work outside the home, and, despite a very different reality, many individuals still believe that middle-income mothers should remain at home. The conflict between a family's goal to be self-sufficient and a woman's responsibility to nurture her children and family remains unresolved and penetrates public policy discussions regularly. Government involvement in the rearing of children is still viewed by some as trespassing into the private lives of its citizens. Child care and early education developed separately, historically, and are still not well integrated. Despite research demonstrating that high-quality ECEC can be beneficial to children, research has also demonstrated that the majority of children in the United States are placed in low-quality care, some of which may be detrimental to the long-term development of children (Helburn, 1995; National Institute of Child Health and Human Development [NICHD], 1998; Whitebook, Howes, & Phillips, 1989).

CURRENT PROVISION OF EARLY CHILDHOOD EDUCATION AND CARE

Now, as in the past, ECEC plays an important role in responding to the complexities and challenges of an advanced industrialized country. ECEC has been a key ingredient for the achievement of social and economic integration across income, ethnic, and racial groups. It assists in the assimilation of immigrants, responds to the changing work roles and composition of families, helps to equalize life opportunities for children of low-income families, and aids in enhancing child development and child well-being generally. Early on, publicly provided early childhood education was designed to accommodate the social needs of vulnerable children, the educational needs of all young children, *and* the needs of working parents. Through the years, the two major functions of care and education have remained separate and often have been viewed as conflicting. One result has been the development of a wide range of programs.

Each type of program has its own objectives, purposes and intended beneficiaries. A variety of programs focused on the development of children are known as ECEC programs. Their aim, typically, is to help young children to take advantage of learning experiences, often with the goal of helping children who have experienced early deprivation and who may have special needs to compensate for early delays and aiding them in becoming ready to learn. Many programs focus on children who come from low-income families and whose parents have had little education. Some of these programs, such as Head Start, provide health and development screenings, stress parent participation, and offer social service assistance. Publicly funded preschool programs typically serve children from disadvantaged families, whereas private preschool programs supported by parent fees are more likely to serve children from all backgrounds and focus more on the child than on providing support to the family. Most often, programs serving 3- to 5-year-olds under the auspices of early childhood education are part-day and part-year programs in centers or schools (Gomby, Larner, Stevenson, Lewit, & Behrman, 1995).

PROGRAM TYPES AND COVERAGE

In 1995, 12.9 million infants, toddlers, and preschool children, or roughly 60% of all children younger than 6 years yet to enter kindergarten, were receiving some type of care other than from their parents on a regular basis (National Center for Education Statistics [NCES], 1996). The type of care a family decides to place their child in is dependent on a family's income, family structure and ethnicity, age of child, maternal education, maternal employment, and parental attitudes toward early care (Hofferth, Brayfield, Deich, & Holcomb,

1991; NICHD, 1998). Low- or middle-income lone mothers or parents working full time may need care beginning when the child is 3 months old or even younger, because the United States has only a brief (3 months), unpaid parental leave at childbirth. (This 12-week job-protected but unpaid leave is provided for through the Family and Medical Leave Act [FMLA] of 1993 [PL 103-3] and covers for employees in firms with more than 50 workers, at the time of pregnancy, childbirth, adoption, or the employees' own illness or that of a family member. Employers can require that employees use their vacation and sick leave before claiming the family leave.)

Child care programs, typically funded and delivered under social welfare auspices, offer full-day care around the year for children from birth through school age. The objective of these programs is to provide care to children while their parents work. Depending on the type of care used by parents, child care may include early education programming. The more formal and skilled the care used, the stronger the emphasis on the cognitive, social, and emotional development of children. Programs that fuse parents' needs for child care with high-quality early childhood education are sometimes explicitly referred to as early childhood care *and* education.

Kindergartens are programs that cover the year before primary school entry, are universal, cover almost all 5-year-olds (those not enrolled are in other preschool programs), and are overwhelmingly delivered under public education auspices. Prekindergarten programs are the form of ECEC that now appears to be increasing most dramatically, largely for 4-year-olds (Schulman et al., 1999). As of 2002, 43 states provide such programs at least in some jurisdictions (Ewen et al., 2002). Only three states (Georgia, New York, and Oklahoma) have statewide prekindergarten programs for all 4-year-olds; only Georgia's is fully implemented. States vary in their provision of full- and part-day kindergarten programs. Part-day programs run for $3\frac{1}{2}$ hours or less, and so-called full-day programs operate for 4–6 hours. About half of all kindergartners attend full-day programs. Two thirds of full-day kindergarten classes were in high-poverty areas, compared with 29% in areas with low poverty rates.

Programs serving children younger than 3 years generally focus on supporting the work efforts of parents. In addition to child care programs, family support programs, sometimes also included with other ECEC programs, offer drop-in child care, information and referral services, weekly or monthly home visits, parenting classes aimed at strengthening parenting skills, and so forth. These family support programs commonly serve families with children younger than 3 years (though these families may include older children), and some programs strive to link services for children with parental supports, such as job training and education. These family support programs target low-income groups and involve a services coordinator to link services that are provided by other community agencies. Typically, these programs rely on public funds and private foundation support and provide services at no charge to their client families. Also typically, these programs target families who are experiencing or who are at risk of poverty, teenage parenthood, or welfare dependency or who are in immigrant groups struggling with acculturation issues (Gomby et al., 1995).

Fifty-six percent of infants younger than 1 year old received nonparental care on a regular basis in 2000 (Phillips & Adams, 2001). Most parents of infants choose informal or in-home care. More than half of American children younger than 1 year old were cared for by a relative, 22% were cared for in family child care homes, and 9% were cared for in center-based care settings (Ehrle, Adams, & Trout, 2001; NICHD Early Child Care Research Network, 1997). Most infants received more than one type of care during their first year of life and were placed in care at 3 months of age, when short-term disability leaves ended or when the unpaid family leave provided under the FMLA was no longer available (NICHD, 1999).

The age at which families place their children in care depends on the work status of the mother, household income, and maternal education. Families more dependent on a mother's income are more likely to place infants in care at an earlier age and use more hours of care than families less dependent on maternal income. Low-income mothers might place their infants in care even earlier than 3 months old. Poor children who are enrolled in center-based programs receive care of the quality equal to affluent children. Poor children who do not enter care by their first birthday are more likely to come from large families, experience persistent poverty, and have mothers with the least education. In contrast, mothers who earned the highest incomes were most likely to place their children between 3 and 5 months old and to use care provided in the home of a nonrelative for the first 15 months (NICHD, 1999).

The preference of parents to have their child cared for by a relative when the child first enters care as an infant shifts toward family child care homes and child care centers after the first year of life (NCES, 1996; NICHD, 1999). Two-year-olds are about equally likely to receive care and education in home-based settings from relatives and nonrelatives but more likely to be cared for in center-based programs when their mothers are working (Ehrle et al., 2001).

By the time a child reaches age 3 years, the parental preference for center-based settings is more striking. NCES (2002) reported that 40.7% of 3-year-olds were enrolled in center-based care in 1995 (see Table 1.4). These rates do vary by family income and mother's education, with higher-income families and college-educated mothers more likely, by far, to enroll their 3-year-olds in a preschool program.

At 4 years of age, the proportion of children enrolled in center-based care grows to 64.7% and to 74.5% by the time children are age 5

Table 1.4. Percentage of children younger than 6 years old in early childhood education and care (ECEC), by type and by age

Characteristic	Children (in thousands)	Total (% in nonparental care)	Type of nonparental arrangement (%)			
			Relative care	Care in nonrelative's home	Center-based program	No nonparental arrangement
TOTAL[a]	21,421	60	21	18	31	40
Age[b]						
Younger than 1 year	4,158	45	24	17	7	55
1 year old	4,027	50	24	19	11	50
2 years old	4,007	54	19	20	19	46
3 years old	4,126	68	21	19	41	32
4 years old	4,065	78	18	15	65	22
5 years old	1,038	84	15	17	75	16

Source: National Center for Education Statistics (NCES; 1996).

Note: Estimates are based on children younger than 6 years old who had yet to enter kindergarten when the NCES data was collected in 1995.

[a]Columns do not add up to the totals because some children participated in more than one type of arrangement.

[b]Age as of December 31, 1994.

(NCES, 2002). When kindergarten and primary school are included, 95% of 5-year-olds are in some form of school or preschool, and of these, more than 75% are in kindergarten. Of some interest, there is no difference in enrollment among Caucasians, African Americans, and Asian Americans, but rates are somewhat lower for Hispanic American children (NCES, 1996, 2002).

Children whose mothers are in the labor force, regardless of whether the work is full time or part time, are more likely to participate in a center-based program than children whose mothers are not in the workforce (39% and 35%, respectively, versus 22%) (NCES, 1997). Working parents seeking full-day child care often combine kindergarten programs with other forms of child care, such as informal or center-based care. Of the 3-year-olds in preschool programs, most are in private preschool programs, but by age 5, the overwhelming majority are in public programs (see Table 1.5).

GOVERNMENT FINANCING OF
EARLY CHILDHOOD EDUCATION AND CARE

The different histories, sources, and levels of public investment perpetuate a false dichotomy in polices for ECEC programs. Table 1.6 summarizes the major federal programs that fund early education and care. It should be noted, however, that fees paid by parents for ECEC in the United States cover about 70% of the operating costs of these programs.

The CCDF provides funding to the states to subsidize the child care expenses of working parents whose family income is less than 85% of the state median income and to subsidize activities related to the improvement of the overall quality and supply of child care in general. Federally, it is administered by the Administration for Children and Families (ACF) in the U.S. Department of Health and Human Services (DHHS). At the state level, it is administered by the agency responsible for social service/welfare administration or employment related activities. In 1998, more than $3 billion was appropriated for this block grant. (See Chapter 3 for further discussion of the CCDF.)

Table 1.5. Enrollment in 2000 of 3- to 5-year-olds in preschool and kindergarten programs by type of program

Age	Total population (in thousands)	Total enrollment		Nursery school		Kindergarten		Length of program day	
		(in thousands)	(as % of total population)	Public	Private	Public	Private	Full-day	Part-day
3 years	3,929	1,541	39.2	644	854	27	16	761	771
4 years	3,940	2,556	64.9	1,144	1,121	227	65	1,182	1,374
5 years	3,989	3,495	87.6	359	206	2,447	484	2,065	1,431
Total for 3–5 years[a]	11,858	7,592	64.0	2,146	2,180	2,701	565	4,008	3,584

Source: National Center for Educational Statistics (NCES; 2002).

[a]Totals may be different than the sum of the data in this table due to rounding of survey data.

Table 1.6. Federal funding for early childhood education and care (ECEC) (in millions)

Program/source	1980	1986	1992	1998	2000
Child Care and Development Block Grant (CCDBG) and Child Care and Development Fund (CCDF)			$825	$3,067	$4,800[a]
Head Start	$766	$1,040	$2,200	$4,355	$5,103
Child and Dependent Care Tax Credit	$956	$3,410	$4,000	$2,485	$3,000
Child and Adult Care Food Program (CACFP)	$239	$501	$1,200	$1,530	$1,740
Social Services Block Grant (SSBG)	$600	$387	$428	$345	$165
Other programs	$246	$146	$877	$888	$5,000
TOTAL	$2,807	$5,484	$9,530	$12,670	$19,808

Sources: Office of Management and Budget (1999); Spar and Gish (1999); U.S. Department of Health and Human Services (DHHS), Administration for Children and Families (ACF), Administration on Children, Youth and Families (ACYF), Child Care Bureau (2002); U.S. House of Representatives (USHR), Committee on Ways and Means (1998).

[a]CCDF funding for 2000 includes $1 billion in spending for child care services under the Temporary Assistance for Needy Families program.

The Child and Dependent Care Tax Credit is a nonrefundable personal income tax credit for expenses related to the care of a dependent child younger than 13 years old or a spouse or dependent who is not able to care for him- or herself because of mental or physical impairment. (The credit can be applied against income tax liability but is of no value to those whose income is below the tax threshold.) As of 2002, the maximum credits were 30% of expenses up to a maximum of $2,400 for one dependent and $4,800 for more than one. For families with higher incomes, the tax limit is reduced to 20% of expenses. As of January 1, 2003, the expense limits will increase to $3,000 for one child/dependent and $6,000 for two or more; the maximum limit will be raised to 35% of expenses. The maximum value of the credit will range between $600 and $1,050 for one child/dependent and between $1,200 and $2,100 for two or more. The tax credit was valued at about $3 billion in 2000, and more than 6 million families received some benefit. The tax credit is administered by the Internal Revenue Service of the U.S. Department of Treasury (USHR, 2000).

Head Start, which began under the general authority of the Economic Opportunity Act of 1964 (PL 88-452), funds direct grants to local programs providing comprehensive early childhood development, educational, health, nutritional, social, and other services primarily to low-income preschool-age children and their families. Most

Head Start programs are part day through the 10-month school year, though some local grantees coordinate with other programs to provide full work-day care. Head Start is federally administered by the Administration on Children, Youth and Families (ACYF) within ACF. It was reauthorized in the Head Start Amendments of 1998 (PL 105-285), funded at $4.3 billion. In federal fiscal year 2001, more than 905,000 children were served, largely 3- and 4-year-olds. More than 55,000 children younger than age 3 are now enrolled in an Early Head Start program.

The Social Services Block Grant (SSBG; Title XX of the Social Security Act, PL 97-35) provides grants to states for social services that most states draw on for at least a portion of their ECEC services. The grants are federally administered by ACF. In federal fiscal year 1997, nearly 13% of SSBG funds were spent on child care services (USHR, 2000). In federal fiscal year 2000, SSBG grants totaled $1.78 billion. In 2000, 43 states reported spending $165 million of SSBG funds for child care.

The Child and Adult Care Food Program provides federal subsidies for breakfasts, lunches, suppers, and snacks meeting federal nutrition requirements that are served in licensed child care centers, schools, and group and family child care homes to children age 12 or younger and for a small number of adults receiving daytime care. It is administered by the U.S. Department of Agriculture's Food and Nutrition Service and was funded at $1.74 billion in federal fiscal year 2001. Through CACFP, approximately 2.6 million children receive nutritious meals and snacks each day as part of the care they receive (U.S. Department of Agriculture, Child and Adult Care Food Program, 2002). At the state level, a variety of agencies administered the program. State agencies made payments to approximately 13,000 child care centers in more than 30,000 sites and to 1,200 family or group child care home sponsors with more than 190,000 homes.

Several other federal programs fund ECEC services. The Education for All Handicapped Children Act of 1975 (PL 94-142) and subsequent associated legislation and amendments, including the Individuals with Disabilities Education Act (IDEA) Amendments of 1997 (PL 105-17), have provided an entitlement to special education services for children ages 3 through 21 with disabilities. Two of the grant programs under IDEA 1997 fund preprimary services. Preschool Grants (in Part B of IDEA 1997) are targeted to programs that serve children ages 3 through 5, and grants for infants and toddlers (in Part C of IDEA 1997) may be used to implement statewide early intervention services for children younger than 3 years and their families.

School districts may also use other categorical federal funds to support preschool education and school age child care in districts serving a high percentage of low-income children. One such program, Even Start, provides grants to schools for family-centered education to help parents of educationally disadvantaged students from birth to 7 years old become full partners in their children's education and to help children gain preliteracy and literacy skills. Funding is also available from the 21st Century Community Learning Centers program for grants to rural and inner-city public schools to address educational and community needs during after-school hours, weekends, and summers.

States complement and sometimes supplement the federal investments in ECEC and have taken a leadership role in developing prekindergarten programs (Schulman et al., 1999). There is wide variation in the number, scope, funding, and programming of state prekindergarten programs across the United States. Most programs serve 4-year-olds who have not yet entered kindergarten, are part-day for the school year, and use education dollars to fund these initiatives. Thirteen states appropriate other state funds to supplement federal Head Start programs. Some states set high quality standards and monitor programs closely, whereas others place quality control at the local level. The scope and depth of programming varies greatly both across and within states, from comprehensive programs promoting health, social, and cognitive development to other programs providing limited opportunities for social interaction and developmental stimulation. In some states, prekindergarten programs are administered by the state's department of education; in others, governance is deferred to local school districts, thus adding further to the variation. Some programs have responded to the needs of working families by extending hours and coordinating with other programs for a full day of programming, or parents have made arrangements for children to be transported to other private programs. Transferring young children from one program to another creates further complexities and is less preferred (Mitchell, Ripple, & Chanana, 1998; Schulman et al., 1999).

Most states that offer prekindergarten do so to help prepare young children for school. Some programs target disadvantaged students, whereas others have opted for a more universal approach. All states use the child's age as one eligibility criterion, and many refer to family income as one of many possible criteria; only 10 restrict eligibility to children from low-income families (Mitchell et al., 1998).

Since 1991, state spending on prekindergarten has expanded from about $700 million to nearly $1.9 billion in 2000, nearly tripling in less than one decade ("Quality Counts," 2002; Schulman et al., 1999). Including state supplements to Head Start would raise these figures even higher. Individual state investments in prekindergarten programs range from $250,000 to more than $200 million annually (Mitchell et al., 1998). Only 7 of the 42 states running prekindergarten programs limit funding to public schools only. Other entities, such as Head Start and child care providers, and other community-based organizations receive prekindergarten funds in 30 states either directly from the states or through a contract with the local public school district. The number of children participating in state-funded prekindergarten programs increased from about 290,000 in 1991–1992 to more than 765,000 in 2000 ("Quality Counts," 2002; Schulman et al., 1999).

In addition to fostering prekindergarten initiatives, states are involved in ECEC in several ways, including tax subsidies for child care and work-related expenses. The total value of the state subsidies in 1994 was estimated to be $175–$350 billion (Stoney & Greenberg, 1996). In 14 states, employer tax credits allowing employers to claim a corporate tax credit of up to 50% of an employee's child care benefits are available but have not been effective in stimulating employer involvement. States also support initiatives to increase the quality and supply of child care programs, such as through start-up and expansion grants, training, licensing and monitoring, and accreditation initiatives.

Local support for early education and care is believed to be significant in some communities, but comprehensive information on funds expended and services provided is not available. In some states, local governments are required to contribute to the cost of child care subsidies, capital improvements and expansions to child care facilities, and prekindergarten costs. Local governments in 26 states contribute to special education and early intervention programs (Stoney & Greenberg, 1996).

States have always carried major responsibility for educational initiatives both with regard to funding and policy-making. It seems that with the enactment of PRWORA in 1996, states are now carrying increased responsibility for the child care needs of low-income families. Since the implementation of PRWORA, the responsibility for designing and implementing ECEC polices under this funding stream has devolved even more to the states. States make the decisions regarding which families will be eligible for and receive subsidy assistance, determine the rates at which providers get paid, determine the extent of parental co-payments in return for receiving child care assistance, and set health and safety standards beyond the minimal federal requirements. States must spend a minimum level of CCDF funding on quality initiatives but are free to spend more, and states have very broad discretion in deciding how to spend their quality dollars.

Although federal funding for ECEC rose substantially in the 1990s, the responsibility for designing and implementing these policies is increasingly falling to the states. It is assumed that states in turn have increased their funding levels, and some states have—but others have not. There are continuing arguments about who is getting assisted and whether it is enough, but there is, in fact, more money in the system than there was even at the end of the 1990s. A study by the U.S. General Accounting Office looked at seven states and found that over the first year after welfare reform legislation was enacted, there had been, on average, a 24% increase in state spending in those states but with significant variation between the states. In one state, spending for child care for low-income families went up by 62%; in another, spending went up by 2% (Greenberg, 1999).

ADMINISTRATIVE RESPONSIBILITIES

ACF, within the DHHS, is responsible for federal programs that promote the economic and social well-being of families, children, individuals, and communities. Several of the agencies reporting to ACF administer many of the programs that fund social welfare–sponsored ECEC and provide financial assistance to states, community-based organizations, and academic institutions to provide services; carry out research and demonstration activities; and undertake training, technical assistance, and information dissemination. The consolidation of child care funding into the CCDBG in 1990 and its reauthorization and expansion as CCDF in 1998 under the auspices of PRWORA was an important step in coordinating the multiple and overlapping child care funding streams.

One agency in ACYF (which is within ACF), the Child Care Bureau, was established in January 1995 to administer federal child care programs to states, territories, and tribes for low-income children and families. The Child Care Bureau has initiated a variety of activities to improve the quality, availability and affordability of child care across the country. The bureau created the National Child Care Information Center to complement, enhance, and promote child care linkages and to serve as a mechanism for supporting quality, comprehensive services for children and families. Information is disseminated to states, territories, and tribes; policy makers; child care organizations; service providers; business communities; parents; and the general public on child care research, funding, and resources through electronic networks, forums, newsletters, and other publications.

Education dollars flowing into early education programs in schools are administered by the U.S. Department of Education. Among the department's priorities are to supplement and complement the efforts of states, local school systems, the private sector, public and private nonprofit educational research institutions, community-based organizations, parents, and students to improve the quality of education.

Other government-sponsored agencies conduct research and administer programs that affect policy making and program development. For example, NICHD is part of the National Institutes of Health, which is part of the DHHS. NICHD conducts research on the reproductive, neurobiological, developmental, and behavioral processes that determine and maintain the health of children, adults, families, and populations. Beginning in 1991, it undertook an ambitious child care study to determine how variations in child care related to child development that has followed more than 1,300 children since birth. Another example is local community discretion to use Community Development Block Grant (CDBG) funds to support local child care centers. The CDBG program is administered by the Department of Housing and Urban Development and channels federal funds to local governments to provide decent housing, provide a suitable living environment, and expand economic opportunities. There are also capital grants available to help finance child care centers that help restore economic viability in designated Empowerment Zones and Enterprise Communities. As discussed previously, income tax credits for child and dependent care expenses are administered by the Internal Revenue Service.

Most programs that channel federal funds to state governments are administered by state counterparts to the federal agencies. Some states have established interagency collaborations similar to those on the federal level to enhance the coordination of early childhood education and policy.

ADVOCACY FOR EARLY CHILDHOOD EDUCATION AND CARE POLICY

Outside of government agencies, hundreds, perhaps even thousands, of private advocacy, think-tank, research, outreach, university, foundation, and public policy institutions in the United States are interested in ECEC policy. Experts at these institutions interact with government officials on a formal and informal basis at privately and publicly sponsored conferences and public hearings and throughout the legislative and budgetary process. Periodically, these experts convene at a national forum to debate issues related to ECEC. For example, in 1997, the White House convened a multidisciplinary, multi-day conference on ECEC. Thousands of publications are available annually on topics related to ECEC.

The efforts at the federal level are mirrored in the individual states and in metropolitan areas. As more responsibility has shifted to the states, states have devolved more policy-making responsibilities to localities. Numerous collaborations among public, voluntary, business, labor, religious, and community agencies have formed at the local level to coordinate social, health, and ECEC services and to advocate, mobilize, and plan. Some collaborations are focused on social needs, and others primarily focus on economic development; and in doing so, both kinds of collaborations take into account the early care and education needs of families.

ECEC is critical to the success of two national priorities in the United States: helping families work and preparing children to succeed in primary school. Welfare reform has driven an unprecedented demand for ECEC services. Despite the increases in federal and state funding (e.g., CCDF, Head Start, special needs, prekindergarten services), demand for these services continues to exceed the supply. Moreover, the existing system capacity and the quality of early childhood programs in the United States are compromised by the lack of affordable quality programs that meet the full-year, full-day needs of working parents and by low staff salaries. Variations in supply and eligibility criteria are likely to grow as public responsibility for how funds should be allocated continues to devolve from the federal government to the states and localities. These limitations on the systems are juxtaposed against the new and widely publicized research on the importance of the first 3 years of life. It is known that the process of learning to read begins well before a child enters primary school and that early experiences critically affect long-term outcomes. The faltering economy may constrain further expansion of federal and state support of early childhood education and care services. The consequences are likely to be felt especially by the young children and families who need help the most.

REFERENCES

Adams, G., & Rohacek, M. (2002). Child care and welfare reform. In A. Weil & K. Finegold (Eds.), *Welfare reform: The next act* (pp. 121–142). Washington, DC: Urban Institute Press.

Barnett, W.S. (1995). Long-term effects of early childhood programs on cognitive and school outcomes. *The Future of Children, 5*(3), 25–50.

Berrueta-Clement, J.R., Schweinhart, L., Barnett, W.S., Epstein, A., & Weikart, D.P. (1984). Changed lives: The effects of Perry Preschool Program on youths through age 19. *Monographs of the High/Scope Educational Research Foundation, No. 8.*

Bowman, B.T., Donovan, M.S., & Burns, M.S. (Eds.). (2001). *Eager to learn: Educating our preschoolers.* Washington, DC: National Academy Press.

Brooks-Gunn, J. (1997). [Commentary]. *Focus, 19*(1), 2.

Bureau of Labor Statistics. (2002a). [Employment status of the civilian noninstitutional population by sex, age, presence and age of youngest child, marital status, race, and Hispanic origin, March 2001 ADF]. Unpublished tables from March 2001 Current Population Survey.

Bureau of Labor Statistics. (2002b). [Labor force status of women by presence and age of youngest child and marital status, annual averages 1994–2001]. Unpublished tables from Current Population Survey.

Carnegie Corporation of New York. (1994). *Starting points: Meeting the needs of our youngest children.* New York: The Carnegie Corporation of New York.

Economic Opportunity Act of 1964, PL 88-452, 42 U.S.C. §§ 2701 *et seq.*

Education Commission of the States. (2001, August; updated 2002, May). *ECS StateNotes: Kindergarten. State statutes regarding kindergarten.* Retrieved August 6, 2002, from http://www.ecs.org/clearinghouse/29/21/2921.pdf

Education for All Handicapped Children Act of 1975, PL 94-142, 20 U.S.C. §§ 1400 *et seq.*

Ehrle, J., Adams, G., & Tout, K. (2001). *Who's caring for our youngest children?: Child care patterns of infants and toddlers.* Washington, DC: Urban Institute Press.

Ewen, E., Blank, H., Hart, K., & Schulman, K. (2002). *State developments in child care, early education, and school-age care: 2001.* Washington, DC: Children's Defense Fund.

Family and Medical Leave Act (FMLA) of 1993, PL 103-3, 5 U.S.C. §§ 6381 *et seq.,* 29 U.S.C. §§ 2601 *et seq.*

Gomby, D.S., Larner, M.L., Stevenson, C.S., Lewit, E.M., & Behrman, R.E. (1995). Long-term outcomes of early childhood programs: Analysis and recommendations. *The Future of Children, 5*(3), 6–24.

Greenberg, M. (1999). *Child care policy two years later.* Washington, DC: Center for Law and Social Policy.

Head Start Amendments of 1998, PL 105-285, 42 U.S.C. §§ 9831 *et seq.*

Helburn, S., et. al. (1995). *Cost, quality and child outcomes in child care centers: Technical report.* Denver: University of Colorado, Department of Economics, Center for Research in Economic Social Policy.

Hofferth, S., Brayfield, A., Deich, S., & Holcomb, P. (1991). *National Child Care Survey, 1990.* Washington, DC: Urban Institute Press.

Individuals with Disabilities Education Act (IDEA) Amendments of 1997, PL 105-17, 20 U.S.C. §§ 1400 *et seq.*

Lazar, I., Darlington, R., Murray, H., Royce, J., & Snipper, A. (1983). *As the twig is bent.* Mahwah, NJ: Lawrence Erlbaum Associates.

Mitchell, A., Ripple C., & Chanana, N. (1998, September). *Prekindergarten programs funded by the states: Essential elements for policy makers.* New York: Families and Work Institute.

National Center for Education Statistics (NCES). (1996, October). *Child care and early education program participation of infants, toddlers, and preschoolers,* NCES 95-824. U.S. Department of Education.

National Center for Education Statistics (NCES). (1997). *Digest of education statistics.* Washington, DC: U.S. Department of Education.

National Center for Educational Statistics (NCES). (2002). *Digest of education statistics, 2001.* Washington, DC: U.S. Department of Education.

National Institute of Child and Human Development (NICHD). (1998). *The childcare network.* Washington, DC: Author.

NICHD Early Child Care Research Network. (1997). Child care in the first year of life. *Merrill-Palmer Quarterly, 43*(3), 340–360.

Office of Management and Budget. (1999). *Budget of the United States government: Fiscal year 2000.* Washington, DC: U.S. Government Printing Office.

Personal Responsibility and Work Opportunity Reconciliation Act of 1996, PL 104-193, 42 U.S.C. §§ 211 *et seq.*

Phillips, D., & Adams, G. (2001). Child care and our youngest children. *The Future of Children, 11*(1), 35–51.

Quality counts 2002: Building blocks for success. (2002, January 10). *Education Week, 21*(17).

Schulman, K., Blank, K., & Ewen, B. (1999). *Seeds of success: State prekindergarten initiatives, 1998–1999.* Washington, DC: Children's Defense Fund.

Shonkoff, J.P., & Phillips, D.A. (Eds.). (2000). *From neurons to neighborhoods: The science of early childhood development.* Washington, DC: National Academy Press.

Smith, S.L., Fairchild, M., & Groginsky, S. (1995). *Early childhood care and education: An investment that works.* Washington, DC: National Conference of State Legislators.

Social Services Block Grant Act, PL 97-35, 42 U.S.C. §§ 303 *et seq.*

Spar, K., & Gish, M.T., (1999). *Child care issues in the 106th Congress* (CRS Report RL30021). Washington, DC: Congressional Research Service.

Stoney, L., & Greenberg, M. (1996). The financing of child care: Current and emerging trends. *The Future of Children, 6*(2), 83–102.

U.S. Department of Agriculture, Child and Adult Care Food Program. (2002). *About CACFP: Why is CACFP important?* Retrieved July 31, 2002, from http://www.fns.usda.gov/cnd/Care/CACFP/aboutcacfp.htm#Why%20CACFP%20Is%20Important

U.S. Department of Health and Human Services, Administration for Children and Families. (2002). *2002 Head Start fact sheet.* Retrieved July, 31, 2002, from http://www2.acf.dhhs.gov/programs/hsb/research/02_hsfs.htm

U.S. Department of Health and Human Services, Administration for Children and Families, Administration on Children, Youth and Families, Child Care Bureau. (2002). Retrieved August 6, 2002, from http://www.acf.dhhs.gov/programs/ccb/research/00acf696/overview.htm

U.S. House of Representatives (USHR), Committee on Ways and Means. (1998). *1998 green book: Background material and data on programs within the jurisdiction of the House Committee on Ways and Means.* Washington, DC: U.S. Government Printing Office.

U.S. House of Representatives (USHR), Committee on Ways and Means. (2000). *2000 green book: Background material and data on programs within the jurisdiction of the*

House Committee on Ways and Means. Washington, DC: U.S. Government Printing Office.

Whitebook, M., Howes, C., & Phillips, D. (1989). *Who cares?: Child care teachers and the quality of care in America. Final report, National Child Care Staffing Study.* Oakland, CA: Child Care Employee Project.

Willer, B., Hofferth, S., Kisker, E., Divine-Hawkins, P., Farquhar, E., & Glantz, F. (1991). *The demand and supply of child care in 1990.* Washington, DC: National Association for the Education of Young Children.

Yoshikawa, H. (1995). Long-term effects of early childhood programs on social outcomes and delinquency. *The Future of Children, 5*(3), 51–75.

2

Defining Program Quality

Debby Cryer

This chapter focuses on one of the main concerns related to early childhood education and care (ECEC) policy in the United States of America: quality in ECEC programs. An introduction to definitions of quality of ECEC services and information on how policy has been directed at meeting the needs of children and families with regard to ECEC programs are provided.

Because ECEC in the United States is a complex system, influenced by political climate and varied cultural groups; represented by strong professional organizations; and consisting of many different types of programs, including profit, nonprofit, public, private, and church-sponsored programs and family child care, there are many stakeholders who have opinions that are considered when identifying quality objectives. In the United States, those representing differing opinions offer much input when quality objectives are identified and prioritized in terms of policy. Although there are some basic similarities among the various definitions of quality, the extent to which specifics are operationalized, used in policy-related issues, or practiced still remains wide ranging.

HOW QUALITY OF EARLY
CHILDHOOD EDUCATION AND CARE IS DEFINED

What is high-quality ECEC? There are certainly a lot of opinions in the United States. We know from research that most parents would tell us that *their own* child is in high-quality ECEC (Cryer & Burchinal,

1997). And ECEC providers would agree, with most saying that they *provide* high-quality care and/or education. However, child advocates, especially those who study the development of children, would disagree, saying that ECEC in the United States is not usually of high quality because it does not sufficiently meet children's developmental needs, nor does it sufficiently protect their health and safety (Helburn, 1995).

In an attempt to define the *quality* of almost any service, it is obvious that subjective values come into play. Just *what* ECEC quality is can be controversial, depending on what aspect of the service is being considered and who is doing the defining. This is certainly true when attempts are made to define quality of ECEC environments, either center-based classrooms or family child care environments (in which care is provided in the provider's own home). Quality of early care and education settings can be defined from many perspectives and can include a variety of indicators. Any definition is likely to be challenged by those with differing priorities or perspectives.

When considering the various definitions of quality of ECEC in the United States, it helps to understand the roots of U.S. early childhood programs, which are discussed in Chapter 1. As in many countries, two primary types of ECEC evolved over many years. The original purpose of *child care* was to provide full-day care for children whose parents, often of lower income groups, worked as part of the labor force. Thus, child care quality was defined in terms of meeting custodial (health and safety) needs of children. The purpose of nursery schools or *preschools* was to provide part-day socialization and educational experiences for young children whose mothers generally were not part of the labor force, so the emphasis in these programs was educational rather than custodial. With the more recent recognition of the importance of the early years for learning, and the huge increase of middle-income women in the workforce, the goals of providing both care and education are being merged.

Within the two types of ECEC now found in the United States (custodial and educational) and within the many programs that now represent some combination of these two types, vastly different quality levels are represented. For example, care aspects of programs might have minimal provisions to maintain children's health and safety or might meet very demanding standards. The same is true with regard to the educational opportunities provided to the children. The levels of quality that stakeholders are willing to accept as high quality depend on the vision that stakeholders have for children, their understandings of how to prepare children to be successful in the society, and the resources available to meet the standards that are set. At present, there is constant pressure from early childhood professionals and many other stakeholders to encourage higher standards in both care and education.

Despite differences between the various stakeholders, however, almost all stakeholders appear to agree on some basic elements. These are the core elements of the professional definition of quality that is widely held in the United States, and most would agree that these are important requirements for quality ECEC programs. These core elements include the following:

- ***Safe care,*** *with sufficient diligent adult supervision that is appropriate for children's ages and abilities, safe toys, equipment, and furnishings*

- ***Healthful care,*** *in a clean environment where sanitary measures to prevent the spread of illness are taken and where children have opportunities for activity, rest, developing self-help skills in cleanliness, and having their nutritional needs met*

- ***Developmentally appropriate stimulation*** *where children have wide choices of opportunities for learning through play in a variety of areas such as language, creativity through art, music, dramatic play, fine and gross motor, [numeracy], and nature/science*

- ***Positive interactions with adults*** *where children can trust, learn from, and enjoy the adults [who] care for and educate them*

- ***Encouragement of individual emotional growth*** *allowing children to operate independently, cooperatively, securely, and competently*

- ***Promotion of positive relationships*** *with other children allowing children to interact with their peers with the environmental supports and adult guidance required to help interactions go smoothly (Cryer, 1999, p. 42)*

Whatever the setting, family child care or care in a center, the same components of quality are thought to be required, although there is room for some flexibility in the details. This is because it is believed that children need the same basics for positive development, whether they are at home, in family child care, or in center-based programs, even though the program activities may be carried out in different ways. For example, the National Association for the Education of Young Children (NAEYC; 1991, 1998) has developed quality criteria for center-based early childhood programs; quality criteria for family child care also exist (Family Child Care Quality Criteria Project, 1995; Modigliani & Bromer, 1997). These documents were developed with input from many constituents in the respective professions. Although center-based ECEC settings and the family child care home might appear to be very different, when the quality definitions for these settings are closely examined, significant overlap can be observed and the themes of the core quality elements just listed are found, with only some of the details differing.

Interestingly, the core quality elements listed previously appear to cross international borders. The points represented in NAEYC's accreditation criteria (1991, 1998) overlap substantially with the view of quality presented in the European Union's ECEC quality definition (Belageur, Mestres, & Penn, 1992) and with the view of quality presented in the *WHO Child Care Facility Schedule* (World Health Organization, Division of Mental Health, 1990). In addition, parents of children in ECEC programs in the United States value similar aspects of quality. Mitchell, Cooperstein, and Larner (1992) reported that parents' views of quality are centered on ensuring their children's health and safety and positive interactions with the ECEC provider. Browne Miller (1990) reported that parents see staff warmth, a good educational program, social activities, and physical activities as being important aspects of quality. Cryer and Burchinal (1997) reported that parents of infants, toddlers, and preschoolers indicated that issues related to health, safety, and adult–child interactions were the most important in terms of quality for their children, and that curriculum aspects were also very important. When considering ECEC quality, however, parents cannot ignore the high importance of accessibility and affordability, which are very realistic concerns. These considerations, however, do not detract from parents' desire for positive experiences for their children while in an ECEC program.

Criticism of the mainstream quality definition is abundant. This ranges from arguments about the inappropriateness of one small detail in the definition to much broader complaints. A good example of the range of criticism found is seen in the responses to NAEYC's version of the widely accepted definition of quality early childhood programs. A major component of NAEYC's definition of quality, known as developmentally appropriate practice (Bredekamp, 1987), has been attacked on many fronts. It has been viewed as being far less relevant for programs serving non-Caucasian cultures than for those serving middle-income Caucasians. For example, Powell (1994) noted that its emphasis on a child-centered teaching approach is at odds with the more didactic teaching that is preferred by many lower-income parents from ethnic minorities. Williams (1994) explained that the child-centered approach, in which the child is encouraged to develop as an individual, also does not apply well to many children raised in Native American cultures, in which the development of the individual is not regarded as important as the relationship of the individual to the group and in which knowledge is seen not to be individually constructed but rather to be socially constructed. Others judge the definition as inadequate in terms of meeting the needs of children with disabilities, who often require more exacting teaching strategies than do typically developing children (Atwater, Carta, Schwartz, & McConnell, 1994).

Despite such criticisms, when the arguments are carefully examined, they are usually found to be focused on relatively small components of the larger construct, not on the core elements. Thus, the definition can sometimes be adapted to incorporate changes, but the core, as a whole, retains its basic identity and does not really change radically. In fact, the concept of developmentally appropriate practice has been revised (Bredekamp & Copple, 1997) to incorporate input from various segments of the profession. It is likely that disagreements about the content of the definition will continue and that ongoing efforts will be required to update the definition in response to input from various critics.

Some opponents reject the mainstream quality definition and offer no sign of a possible compromise in viewpoint. Moss (1994) argued that early childhood program quality is a relative concept, not an objective reality, and that definitions change over time, according to values, beliefs, needs, and other requirements of the various stakeholders involved. Thus, quality must be continually redefined, and only through a process of definition will any result be accepted by the constituents for whom it was created. This relativistic approach questions the validity of the mainstream quality definition, and at the extreme, whether there can ever be agreement on any one definition. Perhaps this perspective can be best understood in terms of how some groups, within what some individuals might label the "religious right" in the United States, seem to view the mainstream definition of quality ECEC. The values held by the religious groups appear to be in substantial conflict with those of the early childhood profession. They emphasize "spare the rod, spoil the child" and ensuring that young children learn religious information rather than the more authoritative, developmental approach that is represented in the mainstream definition. An adaptation to the mainstream definition to incorporate these values seems much less possible, although it is still likely that a definition of quality developed by such religious groups might overlap with the mainstream definition in some areas, such as health or safety.

Children have not often been included as stakeholders who help define the quality of their programs. If a measure of children's happiness counts in this regard, however, it is useful to know that children in higher quality programs (as determined by a professional definition), demonstrate more positive feelings about ECEC than do their peers who are in lower quality programs (Peisner-Feinberg & Burchinal, 1995).

TYPES OF QUALITY THAT ARE DEFINED

In a discussion about assessing quality of ECEC programs in the United States, an understanding of the two different types of quality that are often referred to in quality discussions (Phillips & Howes,

1987) is helpful. *Process quality* consists of those aspects of an ECEC setting that children actually experience, such as teacher–child and child–child interactions; the types of spaces, activities, and materials available to children; and how everyday personal care routines, such as meals, toileting, and rest, are handled. Children directly experience these processes, which are thought to have an influence on their well-being and developmental outcomes (Peisner-Feinberg & Burchinal, 1997; Whitebook, Howes, & Phillips, 1989).

Structural quality consists of the framework that allows process quality to occur—factors that influence the processes that children actually experience. These characteristics are part of the setting used by children and also the environment that surrounds that setting, such as a center or community. Examples of structural quality characteristics include measures of group size, adult–child ratios, and education and experience of the teachers or director of a program. Originally, structural quality variables represented only aspects of ECEC considered amenable to regulation (Phillips & Howes, 1987). The definition has expanded, however, to include variables, such as staff wages, teacher turnover, or parent fees, that are not considered amenable to regulation in the system of ECEC that presently exists in the United States (Phillipsen, Burchinal, Howes, & Cryer, 1997).

DEFINITIONS OF
QUALITY USED IN REGULATION

Child care licensing regulation usually consists primarily of specified objectives for structural quality in ECEC programs. At present, licensing of ECEC programs is set and enforced by each of the states. These regulations usually include requirements regarding numbers of children allowed per teacher, space, general sanitation, nutrition, building inspection, teacher training and qualifications, prevention of child neglect or abuse, emergency procedures, and health of children and staff. In some cases, regulations might also include requirements for classroom materials or practices, but this is less usual. Regulation is established as part of a political process, with input from many stakeholders representing different interests. Generally, an attempt is made to balance the needs of children with the costs of meeting the regulation and the ability of the families, ECEC programs, and the greater society to bear those costs.

Although licensing regulation is thought to represent only the basics required for quality, just *what* is considered to be basic varies substantially by state. In some states, usually in the less economically advantaged regions of the country, regulation is less stringent than in more economically advantaged states. For example, the number of infants (from birth to 12 or 18 months of age) allowed per adult is a good gauge of how stringent a state's ECEC licensing regulation is. In 1999, regulation in Alabama and New Mexico allowed one adult to care for up to six infants at a time, whereas in California, one adult could care for only three infants (National Resource Center for Health and Safety in Child Care, 1999). Alabama and New Mexico tend to have very lax regulation for ECEC; regulation in California is much more demanding.

The stringency of licensing regulation changes according to the political and economic climates in the various states. During liberal administrations, standards are more likely to become more stringent, whereas during conservative administrations, the opposite tends to be true. Standards have become somewhat more stringent since the early 1990s in many states, but changes are generally not extreme. North Carolina, a state with large numbers of children in ECEC and many mothers, with children younger than 5 years, in the work force, provides a reasonable picture of how standards have become more stringent. In the 1970s, there was no child care regulation in North Carolina. In the 1980s, regulation had been enacted, but it was extremely lax (e.g., allowing 1 adult for every 9 infants). Since the 1990s, requirements for teacher qualifications and playground safety have become more demanding, and the adult–child ratios have continued to improve, eventually moving to 5 infants per caregiver.

It should be noted that regulation, although present in all states at some level, is not always applied to all ECEC programs. For example, in many states, no regulation applies to part-day programs or to church-affiliated child care programs, whereas in some states some programs are exempt from some of the standards. When one considers that the state standards are supposed to represent basic protections for children, it is evident that many children do not receive any protection from the state at all. This is due to decisions encouraged by the various stakeholders. Most states indicate that although they provide through regulation the basic protections for children in child care, it is up to children's parents to guarantee that their children receive the quality of care and education that the parents believe to be necessary. Parents with young children, however, are often at the point of their lowest income-earning potential and cannot afford to spend more than they already do on child care, which is most often not highly subsidized by the government in the way that public schools or public institutions of higher education are. Thus, parents, who are actually the consumers of child care (although it is their children who experience the care), are not likely to lobby for higher standards that will require them to pay additional costs.

DEFINITIONS OF PROCESS QUALITY

Definitions of quality that include processes—what children actually experience—have largely been avoided in terms of regulation but have been developed in the U.S. early childhood profession for several purposes, such as measuring quality for program improvement, voluntary accreditation, or for research on the effects of quality on children's development. Various measures used to specify and evaluate the mainstream definition of ECEC process quality have been developed since the 1980s. Well-known examples include the Early Childhood Environment Rating Scale–Revised Edition (ECERS-R; Harms, Clifford, & Cryer, 1998), the Infant/Toddler Environment Rating Scale (ITERS; Harms, Cryer, & Clifford, 1990), the Family Day Care Rating Scale (FDCRS; Harms & Clifford, 1989), the NAEYC (1985, 1991, 1998) accreditation guides, and the Observational Record of the Caregiving Environment (NICHD Early Child Care Research Network, 1996). Each represents a version of process quality that is assumed to produce specific child outcomes. Some have been used in research, whereas others were designed to evaluate and improve program quality. All procedures require direct observation of children and adults in ECEC settings during times of child activity. In addition, a staff interview or review of documents to collect information on unobserved requirements is often used to supplement observations. One type of measure, a global process quality assessment, is used to document the overall physical and learning quality of an ECEC environment instead of making more specific assessments of quality.

In the development of these instruments, the primary stakeholders involved were members of the early childhood profession. Certainly, the instrument that received the most input from the greatest number of stakeholders is the one developed by NAEYC (1985) for its accreditation program. In developing this instrument, members of the organization, including practitioners, policy makers, parents, educators, and researchers, had the opportunity to provide input. The instrument has been revised (1991, 1998) on the basis of continued and changing input from the field; similarly, the ECERS-R is an update of an earlier version (Harms & Clifford, 1980).

STATUS OF PROGRAM
QUALITY AND EFFECTS ON CHILDREN

In attempting to determine the status of ECEC in the United States in terms of process quality, findings have shown that good care is rarely found. In addition, there is great variation in the quality found, with some few programs providing very good ECEC and many others providing much lower quality.

The Cost, Quality and Child Outcomes Study (Helburn, 1995), for example, used combined scores from several process quality assessments and concluded that care provided in most centers in the United States is of poor to mediocre quality, with infant and toddler care being of the poorest quality. Poor quality care, which characterized almost half of the infant and toddler rooms studied, represented problems in basic sanitary conditions related to diapering and feeding; safety problems; lack of warm, supportive relationships with adults; and lack of materials required for physical and intellectual growth. Most older preschoolers in child care experienced mediocre care, which is defined as care in which children's basic needs for health and safety were met, with some warmth and support provided by adults, and with some learning experiences offered. These findings are similar to those of other studies using process quality assessment in other states, in which average quality levels were also rarely seen in the good range (Scarr, Eisenberg, & Deater-Deckard, 1994; Whitebook et al., 1989).

Family child care study results tend to be similar to those found for center-based care. A major study of family child care (Galinsky, Howes, Kontos, & Shinn, 1994) used several process quality assessments. In this study, it was found that few homes (only about 9%) had high scores, the majority (56%) fell into the adequate/custodial range, and a substantial number (35%) were scored as being of low quality.

As structural quality varies across states, so does process quality. Studies have shown that states with the least stringent regulation tend to have more ECEC programs that are determined to have low process quality (Helburn, 1995; Whitebook et al., 1989).

From a more international perspective, quality of ECEC programs in the United States has been compared with programs serving children of similar ages in Austria, Germany, Portugal, and Spain (Tietze, Cryer, Bairrão, Palacios, & Wetzel, 1996). On average, all of these other countries were found to provide care that was less than "good" in terms of the process quality measure that was used in all countries. However, the range of quality found in the United States, from very poor to very good, was far wider than the range found in other countries, where ECEC resources appeared to be distributed across the population more equitably.

The validity of the mainstream definition of process quality has increased with results of research since the 1980s (e.g., Galinsky et al., 1994; Helburn, 1995; Roupp, Travers, Glantz, & Coelen, 1979; Whitebook et al., 1989). This research has examined variations in child care quality with reference to the mainstream ECEC quality definition. The focus on the research has been to determine the status of ECEC program quality in the United States, to examine the relationships between structural quality variables and process quality, and to present the implications of varying quality in terms of children's well-being. Most of the research has defined children's positive outcomes in terms of the developmental areas that are associated with future school success, with the assumption that school success will lead to greater chances for adult success in the majority society. The Cost, Quality and Child Outcomes Study found that the quality of child care experienced during the preschool years continued to have an effect on children's outcomes, even at the end of second grade (Peisner-Feinberg et al., 1999).

INCORPORATION OF PROCESS QUALITY DEFINITIONS INTO POLICY

With the results of child care quality research and a greater understanding of the importance of early experiences in terms of brain development, there has been a move to incorporate process quality requirements into regulation of child care programs. The U.S. Army and Navy were early participants in this movement, requiring first that their centers and family child care homes meet certain standards on the ECERS and its revision, the ITERS, and the FDCRS and later that programs meet standards for accreditation by the appropriate national professional organizations. In addition, some states began to provide higher subsidy payments to programs that met higher process quality standards, especially those for accreditation by NAEYC. The state of North Carolina has passed regulations that require all licensed child care programs to be rated according to a five-star system to clearly indicate levels of quality for consumers. The lowest quality level (one star) of the system represents existing baseline regulations and is required of any licensed program. The higher levels (two to five stars), however, are voluntary, and require programs to meet higher requirements of staff qualifications and to meet specified standards for process quality, measured by the ECERS-R, ITERS, and FDCRS, when applying for the highest numbers of stars. Other states are also implementing this type of system, which incorporates a measure of process quality into licensing regulation

Because of the relatively weak involvement by the federal government regarding the movement toward higher quality in ECEC programs, attention by child advocates has been directed primarily at the states. It should be noted that federal funds often contribute to the funding of quality improvement initiatives. Several states have led the way in moving toward higher quality child care for all children. North Carolina, with its Smart Start programs, may be the best example of a state in which substantial efforts and the funding to support them are being made to upgrade the quality of care that young children receive. The Smart Start program provides funds to local associations, usually at the county level, whose proposals for use of funds in the region has been accepted. Members of these associations, called Smart Start Partnerships, include stakeholders with various interests who all share a concern for the well-being of young children. The funds can be used for a variety of purposes to improve the situations of young children, but much attention has been given to upgrading child care programs. Decisions about how funds are to be used are made at the local level with input from various stakeholders. An evaluation of Smart Start (Bryant, Bernier, Maxwell, & Peisner-Feinberg, 2002) indicated that the Smart Start program is most effective in increasing the quality of child care when more funds are targeted for this purpose.

Other states, especially those with less stringent regulations, are also improving the quality of child care in various ways. For example, Arkansas has a program in which parents receive higher tax credits when their children are enrolled in ECEC centers that voluntarily meet higher standards. Centers that voluntarily meet higher standards can receive some financial help and consultation from the state to upgrade the services they provide. A few of the other states involved in innovative attempts to upgrade quality include Colorado, Oklahoma, and Georgia.

SUMMARY

The definition of ECEC quality has been relatively stable in the United States since the mid-1970s; since then there has been enormous growth in ECEC services. The basics are generally agreed on, and the details continue to be refined, based on stakeholder values and opinions. Although the definition of quality has been "alive and well," the actual implementation of this definition into the ECEC practices that children experience and that have a direct, lasting effect on children's development has lagged far behind. Research continues to show that high quality in ECEC programs is the rarity rather than the norm, especially for infants and toddlers. Many states are working to improve the quality of ECEC that children receive, using innovative methods and clearly stated requirements that include the definition of process quality. The necessary balance, however, between meeting children's developmental needs for protection, learning, and positive relationships and providing programs that parents can afford for their children, although improving, has not yet been found. We look to this millennium for the discovery of this balance.

REFERENCES

Atwater, J., Carta, J., Schwartz, I., &. McConnell, S. (1994). Blending developmentally appropriate practice and early childhood special education: Redefining best practice to meet the needs of all children. In B.L. Mallory & R.S. New (Eds.), *Diversity and developmentally appropriate practices: Challenges for early childhood education* (pp. 185–201). New York: Teachers College Press.

Belageur, I., Mestres, J., & Penn, H. (1992). *Die Frage der Qualität in Kinderbetreuungseinrichtungen (Diskussionspapier)* [Quality of child care centers (A discussion paper)]. Brussels, Belgium: Kommission der Europäischen Gemeinschaften.

Bredekamp, S. (1987). *Developmentally appropriate practice in early childhood programs serving children from birth through age 8.* Washington, DC: National Association for the Education of Young Children.

Bredekamp, S., & Copple, C. (Eds.). (1997). *Developmentally appropriate practice in early childhood programs* (Rev. ed.). Washington, DC: National Association for the Education of Young Children.

Browne Miller, A. (1990). *The day care dilemma: Critical concerns for American families.* New York: Kluwer Academic/Plenum.

Bryant, D., Bernier, K., Maxwell, K., & Peisner-Feinberg, E. (2002). *Smart Start and child care in North Carolina: Effects on quality and changes over time.* Chapel Hill: University of North Carolina, Frank Porter Graham Child Development Institute.

Cryer, D. (1999, May). Defining and assessing early childhood program quality. *The Annals of the American Academy of Political and Social Science, 563,* 39–55.

Cryer, D., & Burchinal, M. (1997). Parents as child care consumers. *Early Childhood Research Quarterly, 12,* 35–58.

Family Child Care Quality Criteria Project. (1995). *Quality criteria for family child care.* Washington, DC: National Association for Family Child Care.

Galinsky, E., Howes, C., Kontos, S., & Shinn, M. (1994). *The study of children in family child care and relative care: Highlights of findings.* New York: Families and Work Institute.

Harms, T., & Clifford, R.M. (1980). *Early Childhood Environment Rating Scale.* New York: Teachers College Press.

Harms, T., & Clifford, R. (1989). *Family Day Care Rating Scale.* New York: Teachers College Press.

Harms, T., Clifford, R., & Cryer, D. (1998). *Early Childhood Environment Rating Scale–Revised Edition.* New York: Teachers College Press.

Harms, T., Cryer D., & Clifford, R. (1990). *Infant/Toddler Environment Rating Scale.* New York: Teachers College Press.

Helburn, S. (Ed.). (1995). *Cost, quality and child outcomes in child care centers: Technical report.* Denver: University of Colorado, Department of Economics, Center for Research in Economic Social Policy.

Mitchell, A., Cooperstein, E., & Larner, M. (1992). *Child care choices, consumer education, and low-income families.* New York: National Center for Children in Poverty.

Modigliani, K., & Bromer, J. (1997). *Quality standards for NAFCC accreditation: Pilot study draft.* Boston: Wheelock College, Family Child Care Study.

Moss, P. (1994). Defining quality: Values, stakeholders and processes. In P. Moss & A. Pence (Eds.), *Valuing quality in early childhood services: New approaches to defining quality* (pp. 10–19). London: Paul Chapman.

National Association for the Education of Young Children (NAEYC). (1985). *Guide to accreditation by the National Academy of Early Childhood Programs.* Washington, DC: Author.

National Association for the Education of Young Children (NAEYC). (1991). *Guide to accreditation by the National Association for the Education of Young Children* (Rev. ed.). Washington, DC: Author.

National Association for the Education of Young Children (NAEYC). (1998). *Guide to accreditation by the National Association for the Education of Young Children: 1998 edition.* Washington, DC: Author.

National Resource Center for Health and Safety in Child Care. (1999). *Individual states' child care licensure regulations.* Aurora, CO: Author.

NICHD Early Child Care Research Network. (1996). Characteristics of infant child care: Factors contributing to positive caregiving. *Early Childhood Research Quarterly, 11,* 269–306.

Peisner-Feinberg, E., & Burchinal, M. (1997). Relations between preschool children's child-care experiences and concurrent development: The Cost, Quality and Outcomes Study. *Merrill-Palmer Quarterly, 43*(3), 451–477.

Phillips, D., & Howes, C. (1987). Indicators of quality in child care: Review of research. In D. Phillips (Ed.), *Quality in child care: What does research tell us?* (pp. 1–19). Washington, DC: National Association for the Education of Young Children.

Phillipsen, L., Burchinal, M., Howes, C., & Cryer, D. (1997). The prediction of process quality from structural features of child care. *Early Childhood Research Quarterly, 12,* 281–303.

Powell, D. (1994). Parents, pluralism, and the NAEYC statement on developmentally appropriate practice. In B.L. Mallory & R.S. New (Eds.), *Diversity and developmentally appropriate practices: Challenges for early childhood education* (pp. 166–182). New York: Teachers College Press.

Roupp, R., Travers, J., Glantz, F., & Coelen, C. (1979). *Children at the center: Final results of the National Day Care Study.* Cambridge, MA: Abt Associates.

Scarr, S., Eisenberg, M., & Deater-Deckard, K. (1994). Measurement of quality in child care centers. *Early Childhood Research Quarterly, 9,* 131–151.

Tietze, W., Cryer, D., Bairrão, J., Palacios, J., & Wetzel, G. (1996). Comparisons of observed quality in early child care and education programs in five countries. *Early Childhood Research Quarterly, 11,* 447–475.

Whitebook, M., Howes, C., & Phillips, D. (1989). *Who cares?: Child care teachers and the quality of care in America. Final report of the National Child Care Staffing Study.* Oakland, CA: Child Care Employee Project.

Williams, L. (1994). Developmentally appropriate practice and cultural values: A case in point. In B.L. Mallory & R.S. New (Eds.), *Diversity and developmentally appropriate practices: Challenges for early childhood education* (pp. 155–165). New York: Teachers College Press.

World Health Organization, Division of Mental Health. (1990). *WHO child care facility schedule with user's manual.* Geneva: Author.

3

Access to Programs

Edna Runnels Ranck

Quality, affordability, and accessibility, three major variables composing early childhood education and care (ECEC), are interwoven to the extent that they have been referred to as the "trilemma of child care." Addressing any one of the three issues without referring to the other two only emphasizes the limited and often inadequate consideration of ECEC services in the United States (Helburn, 1999; Morgan, 1998; National Education Association, 1998). Rather, all three must be addressed simultaneously when determining program operations, professional development practices, family involvement opportunities, and public policy efforts. In this chapter, affordability is considered an element of accessibility.

Having access to ECEC should mean that the needs of both families and children are addressed. All parents should have a choice among a variety of programs that meet their needs for location, hours of care, friendly and competent staff, curriculum content, and stability and reliability of care at a cost that is within the family budget. At the same time, the program must also meet the developmental needs of all children for an appropriate, caring, and stimulating environment that emphasizes both education and nurture and addresses any special needs. In light of the amalgam of market and managed ECEC programs available in the United States, meeting the access criteria can be a daunting task for parents at all socioeconomic levels. The search often is particularly difficult for low-income working families and especially for parents in the process of leaving the welfare rolls (Cahan, 1989; Helburn, 1999).

It should be noted that parents are not always left entirely on their own to figure out the nature of the local ECEC structure. Parents talk with family members and friends, check the job-wanted advertisements, search the yellow pages, talk with human resources staff in their workplace, and visit ECEC programs in their area. Many families throughout the United States are counseled by trained personnel in the local child care resource and referral (CCR&R) agency. Even assistance from any or all of these sources, however, does not guarantee finding and selecting the kind of care that parents want and children need.

The characteristics of ECEC, including access, are linked to the basic economic, social, and political nature of the country in which the children and families live. The United States, as a pluralistic society with a democratic government and overlapping roles for one federal, many state, and thousands of local government structures, is also subject to a continuum of attitudes toward child rearing. Attitudes based on the belief systems of families and the nation ultimately determine both the kind of systems that develop and the style of consensus building that creates policy.

To understand the nature of ECEC access issues in the United States, it helps to recognize the range of perceptions that shape factors affecting ECEC programs. In particular, the roles and responsibilities of parents and families in contrast with those of governments are critical:

> *Most voters conclude that access to care is not a very big problem. Rather they assume the real problem is being able to afford the care [actually another form of access issue] and as such think there are alternative options that do not rely solely on government which should be explored: companies, churches, elderly, flex time and schools. (Lake Research, Inc., 1996, p. 6)*

In contrast, Barbara R. Bergmann, professor emeritus of economics at the American University and the University of Maryland, College Park, wrote that making "[child] care of acceptable quality 'affordable' for millions of American families" would cost tens of billions of dollars and that "costs of these magnitudes preclude financing of any significant part by employers or philanthropies" (p. 208).

Clearly, addressing the issues of access to ECEC programs requires an understanding of the programmatic and political aspects of the field. The problems inherent in the delivery of ECEC programs and services in the United States are best viewed through the dual lenses of the historical development of supply and the wide-ranging and often erratic demand for services.

SUPPLY OF AND DEMAND FOR EARLY CHILDHOOD EDUCATION AND CARE

The history of ECEC program access, beginning in the United States in the 19th century, has largely been based on persistent sets of dichotomies:

- *Custodial child care versus early childhood education:* Who receives services of what type and curriculum design? What are the goals and objectives of individual ECEC programs?

- *Women, especially mothers, at home with children versus women in the paid work force:* Who provides care for the children, who gets paid for the services provided, and who pays for the services?

- *Governments versus the private sector (families, employers, religious institutions, and philanthropies):* What are the sources for the fiscal and in-kind resources to design, build, house, and operate ECEC programs?

- *Crisis conditions with limited federal government support for ECEC versus universal support for all children:* When is it acceptable for the government to support ECEC? When is it not acceptable?

Data on supply of ECEC have been collected by major national research organizations, notably the U.S. General Accounting Office (1989, 1998), the research arm of the U.S. Congress, and the Urban Institute, a national research organization (Capizzano, Adams, & Sonenstein, 2000). In 1996, the National Association of Child Care Resource and Referral Agencies (NACCRRA) reported on ECEC supply data (Adams, Foote, & Vinci, 1996) and will update these data in 2002. At the end of 1999, The Enterprise Foundation released a guide to collecting community ECEC supply-and-demand data (Smith, n.d.). The collected data provide some of the following information about access to ECEC in the United States.

Preschool/Kindergarten

Historically, and to a large extent even in the present, ECEC programs outside the public school system in the United States focus on children in the 3- to 5-year-old age bracket. Kindergartens for 5-year-olds, now a part of virtually every American public school, originated in the 19th century as separate programs for children prior to the compulsory age for education. These early forms of kindergarten and day nurseries, later to be called day care and then child care centers, often emphasized the improvement of children and families via preschool education. Nursery schools, originally viewed as laboratory schools in colleges and universities, were identified as a necessary component of every middle-income child's early upbringing. Today, a wide array of center-based programs proliferates in the struggle to meet the rapidly growing need for ECEC at every socioeconomic level. All states require ECEC centers to be licensed, although the licensing requirements vary widely among the 50 states and the District of Columbia and some programs are exempt from regulations (U.S. General Accounting Office, 1998).

Other Types of Care

The picture for ECEC services to other age groups is not as optimistic. Data show an increased need for infant and toddler care (Shonkoff & Phillips, 2000) and appropriate school-age, out-of-school programs (Capiazzano, Adelman, & Stagner, 2002; Gootman, 2000). In addition, care during nontraditional working hours and for children with mild illness is a growing concern for working parents. Both historical and current reasons have produced these changed needs: The preschool programs of the past served 3- to 5-year-olds for limited periods during the academic year. Younger children were not enrolled in out-of-home programs at all, and most slightly older children attended only part time. As the number of mothers entering the work force expanded rapidly and steadily during the later decades of the 20th century, the number of available full-time programs for very young and school-age children continued to expand significantly (Bowman, Donovan, & Burns, 2001).

Family Child Care

One perceived solution to the shortage of care for very young children was the expansion of the number of family child care (FCC) homes nationwide. FCC, the care of no more than five or six children in the private home of a provider, appeared to be a quick, easy, and inexpensive way to address the ECEC supply issue, especially for the care of infants and toddlers. FCC development, however, requires a pool of appropriate, available, and willing individuals able to operate a small business for up to 60 hours a week and design an appropriate curriculum for children of varied ages in a private residence. FCC providers today are often professionally trained, are members of a network of providers and a national organization, and are participants in the Child and Adult Care Food Program, administered by the Food and Nutrition Service of the U.S. Department of Agriculture. State regulations for FCC providers vary even more than those for center-based programs, but most states have some requirements in place.

School-Age Child Care

Elementary school children with working parents require care before and after school hours and during illnesses, school holidays, vacations, and emergencies. School-age children in the not-too-distant past left school around 3:00 in the afternoon to go home unsupervised or to be looked after by relatives. During the 1970s and 1980s, private programs for school-age child care (SACC) emerged, and today the demand for SACC (care provided outside of school hours) is a major focus of public schools in many states. In addition, both government and the private sector have become involved in developing quality SACC in part through an accreditation program (Román, 1998). The part-time nature of SACC, the resistance of older elementary-age children to "child care," and the link between juvenile crime statistics and use of SACC all suggest the need to address more closely the wide variety of SACC access issues.

The likelihood of a mismatch between supply and demand occurs when the supply is inadequate, inappropriate, or unaffordable and when the demand does not synchronize with the programming that exists. Even if the numbers, however, correspond between supply and demand at the state or community level, the likelihood of a mismatch remains if supply characteristics such as location, schedule, enrollment, program philosophy, and cost do not mesh with the demand requirements of parents and families.

Such discrepancies persist at the community level and within the profession itself when the strengths and weaknesses of a given ECEC delivery system are caught up among the differences between market systems (e.g., most private center- and home-based ECEC programs) and managed systems (e.g., Head Start, military child care, public schools). Changes required in the quality and quantity of service delivery required to meet the variables of age, work schedule, income, fees, and developmental characteristics of children are vast in any given community. However, the planning role of CCR&R agencies in conjunction with the willing participation of all types of ECEC programs, local and state governments, school districts, employers, and parents, often offers the opportunity to focus on what exists in a community and what is needed in the short- and long-term to meet the needs for ECEC.

PARENTAL CHOICE

Parents' search and selection of an ECEC program is the nexus between supply and demand. Although in some types of ECEC, the match between supply and demand is more balanced in terms of access, parents have other demands in regard to what they want for their children. Frequently, parents must choose among the limited options available where they reside, whereas in another community, even one that is close by, the choice may be wider. Choices among ECEC options for all parents, regardless of family income, are determined by a broad range of characteristics:

- The location, number, and variety of center- and home-based programs in relation to family's home and the parents' places of employment
- Variations in ECEC options in urban, suburban, and rural areas
- Enrollment capacity and waiting list size
- Provision of care for children with mild illness
- Tuition charged to cover operating costs of the program
- Subsidy issues: eligibility for a subsidy, availability of a subsidy, and the size of the parental co-payment
- Availability of transportation to and from the program; possession of an automobile; ability to car-pool; and availability, cost of, and access to public transportation
- Compatibility of child-rearing and educational philosophy between the family and the program
- Compatibility of developmentally appropriate curriculum and developmental stage of the child and cultural background

The range of variables reflecting the nature of ECEC may or may not be perceived as barriers. Clearly, income level is critical because of the possible need for a subsidy or the ability to provide one's own transportation. For example, income and scheduling requirements in Head Start limit enrollment to very economically disadvantaged children for less than a full-day, full-year program. Insufficient funding to cover the costs for all eligible children is another factor in parental choice. Efforts are underway in many communities to lift those eligibility restrictions, including a growing number of collaborative efforts between Head Start and ECEC programs. In addition, in school districts and communities in many states, the role of public schools in the provision of ECEC for children younger than kindergarten age is expanding. A real or perceived lack of cooperative experience between public schools and the private ECEC sector, especially Head Start, with philosophical differences and the ECEC field's fear of loss of control over program development and operation, all contribute to the turmoil in serving young children in the United States (Children's Defense Fund, 1999).

PUBLIC ENTITLEMENTS TO INCREASE ACCESS

One obvious solution to the ECEC access issue would be to make ECEC an entitlement. ECEC as a statutory entitlement is available, however, only under highly specific, limited and largely temporary conditions based on a range of politically determined factors, some at the federal level and others at the state or local levels. The services described next represent policy decisions made in a pluralistic society with a democratic form of government, in which policy making is by design distributed among a variety of power sources. Consensus and implementation occur only at the end of a complex series of decisions and compromises, including the appropriation and allocation of funds and related resources. Resistance to making ECEC an entitlement in the United States, except for in crisis conditions, continues to operate at all government levels (Helburn & Bergmann, 2002).

Welfare

When parents on welfare leave the welfare rolls to enter the work force, states guarantee subsidized ECEC for a designated period (as of 2002, 1 or 2 years), if needed, for children younger than 13 years old and for dependents with disabilities. Other low-income working parents may also be eligible for a subsidy (payment) for ECEC care but only within the limits of available funds. Payment goes to contracted community-based ECEC programs or occurs through vouchers payable to the parent or provider. A parent co-payment, usually calculated on a sliding fee scale based either on the federal poverty level or on the state's median income, is generally required. Total funding therefore comes from a combination of federal and state dollars and the parent's co-payment.

Child Protective Services

Although there is no federal requirement that children under the supervision of the state for reasons of abuse or neglect have access to ECEC, states may choose to set such a policy.

Special Needs

Under provisions of federal legislation such as the Individuals with Disabilities Education Act (IDEA) Amendments of 1997 (PL 105-17), children diagnosed with a handicapping condition or disability are eligible for limited services often provided through a public school, often called a local education agency. In addition, children from birth to age 3 years who are diagnosed with a disability or who are found to be at risk of significant developmental delay qualify for early intervention services. Funding comes from combined federal, state, and local sources and may include federal dollars given to states as part of the Child Care and Development Fund (CCDF) which is described later in this chapter and in Chapter 1.

Prekindergarten

States have the option to establish prekindergartens based on legislation, but the final decision to offer kindergarten usually rests with the local school district. Most school districts in the United States offer half- or full-day kindergarten for children 1 year younger than the compulsory age of education, usually established by statute at 6 or 7 years of age (see Table 1.1 in Chapter 1). If a district chooses to offer prekindergarten for 3- and 4-year-olds, all children living in the district must be able to enroll. Schools may also contract with ECEC programs in the community to provide prekindergarten. Funds are provided by the school district and may include federal and state funds allocated to the school district and to the child care government agency appointed by the governor to administer CCDF funds.

Head Start

Though a discretionary grant program and not an entitlement, Head Start funds provided full- or part-day comprehensive services to more than 900,000 young children in fiscal year 2002. (An entitlement program must accept all eligible children who wish to participate in the program, whereas a discretionary grant sets a cap on enrollment based on funding limits, thereby creating possible waiting lists among eligible participants.) Many Head Start programs have begun working with other ECEC programs and public schools to expand both the level and length of service. Decisions about ECEC, except for Head Start, rest with the local school district with varying amounts of input from the state's department of education. ECEC services and programs funded through the state's department of human services generally use a combination of federal funds given to states as part of the CCDF or the Child and Adult Care Food Program and state funds. Head Start's funding comes directly from the federal government, although some states fund selected services for children eligible for Head Start.

POLICIES TO ENCOURAGE ACCESS TO SERVICES

Despite the very limited availability of ECEC entitlements in the United States and resistance to making ECEC an across-the-board entitlement (Helburn & Bergmann, 2002), efforts to expand access to ECEC programs are in place at every governmental level, though these efforts are not necessarily comparable among localities or states. In 1990, and with reauthorization in 1996, the federal government implemented the Child Care and Development Block Grant (CCDBG), which is now combined with other funding streams and is also called the Child Care and Development Fund (CCDF). These block grants give federal funds to states to subsidize ECEC according to state-determined eligibility and time limits. The funds help defray child care costs not only for families on welfare but also for low-income working families that are at risk of needing welfare.

Although a percentage of the funds is allocated to each state to pay for child care vouchers or to contract with existing ECEC programs, funding is designed to allow parents to choose the type of care they want, including nonregulated care by relatives and friends. Other CCDF funds (4% of the total CCDF state grant) are directed by the states to provide for "quality services," which may include professional development, supply-building, and loans and grants for improved and expanded services. States are required to submit a spending plan to the federal government and to report periodically on the status of the spending.

States may also spend state funds on ECEC; some of these funds must be used to match, or draw down, the federal money. Innovative states have used their resources to fund new services for families and to encourage cooperative ventures among the various agencies that provide ECEC (Stebbins, 1998). In some cases, the expansion of public schools into ECEC service delivery is perceived as a barrier because of the impact on the ECEC programs already operating in the community. In addition, general public school hours do not meet the needs of working parents for the supervision of their children. Public schools, however, may contribute access advantages through their available funding, facilities, and educated staff (Marx & Seligson, 1988).

A set percentage of the CCDF funds has specifically established or expanded school-age care and CCR&R services for designated geographical areas in states. CCR&R agencies that give referrals or administer CCDF vouchers must inform eligible parents, including those going off welfare, about all types of available ECEC so that no type of care is implied by the wording used or by the tone of voice as better or worse than any other. In addition to managing federal subsidy dollars, CCR&R agencies also address supply-and-demand issues, offer staff and board training and technical assistance, facilitate collaboration among members of the ECEC service delivery system, and work with planning entities on ECEC projections. CCR&R agencies play a key role at the local, state, and national levels in collecting, analyzing, and disseminating data about the field, although, again, the role varies among the states.

Other ECEC policies have been directed to meet the needs of families with children with special physical, emotional, and cognitive/developmental needs. Children evaluated by local school child study teams and mental health professionals are referred for services in the most appropriate, natural environment, which is sometimes described as the least restrictive environment. Center- and home-based ECEC programs are encouraged to enroll children with special needs, and most find the practice beneficial to all children in the program. Efforts to give support to staff working with special needs children are encouraged, especially in programs without funds budgeted for such services.

The Map to Inclusion Project, sponsored by the U.S. Department of Health and Human Services, operated for several years in approximately 25 states. Its goal was to establish a state plan for children with special needs in ECEC (Map to Inclusive Child Care Institute, 1999). Some states continue with the original mapping model using their own funds.

Head Start offers health and mental health services to enrolled children and their families. Staff training enables on-the-job supervision in working with special needs children (Final Rule–Head Start Program Performance Standards, 1996). Through federal funding from Title I of the Elementary and Secondary Education Act of 1965 (PL 89-10) and subsequent reauthorizations and associated laws, including the No Child Left Behind Act of 2001 (PL 107-110), eligible public schools with a low-income population provide a range of services to children who meet program and residency requirements.

BARRIERS TO UNIVERSAL ACCESS

Limited entitlements and a slowly growing support effort for ECEC create positive, family-friendly policies. Further along the ECEC policy continuum, however, barriers emerge that affect access to ECEC services. Exclusion from programs for any reason defeats the possibility of universal ECEC available to all children; practices that further limit access are set by regulation, program policies, and economic restrictions against quality programming (Cost, Quality and Child Outcomes Study Team, 1995).

The main barriers to equitable access to any type of ECEC are the restrictions that limit services to a specified category of children. These largely artificial boundaries include the age of the child, family residency, parental income and participation in the work force, program operating schedules, a child's physical or mental abilities, and the availability of funds to cover the program costs of all eligible children. Another challenge to ensuring access to high-quality ECEC programs is the range of staff professional preparation and continuing education opportunities, usually the result of low compensation and high staff turnover (Whitebook & Bellm, 1999). Although some ECEC leaders claim that regulations limiting group size and child–adult ratios are barriers to full enrollment, many of these leaders' colleagues believe that the health, safety, and developmental growth of young children require a small group size and age-appropriate ratio between children and adults.

Among the most significant access barriers are those dictated by the nature of the U.S. political system, in which the private individual retains certain rights and in which the states are expected and required to make critical decisions affecting families and educational programs. Local or "home rule" for public schools and municipal and county taxes and zoning requirements hold a paramount position in American governance. Each state can and usually does develop differing sets of ECEC regulations, policies, and procedures. Furthermore, the trust level is often low between proponents of federal control and supporters of states' rights (Adams & Poersch, 1994, 1996; U.S. General Accounting Office, 1998).

Ultimately, societal attitudes and underlying assumptions about children and families prevail and are by definition barriers to easy decision making. Responses to such questions as the following are articulated strongly along a liberal–conservative continuum:

- Who is responsible for rearing the children?

- How are the children to be socialized and educated, who does the socializing and educating, and for what fundamental purposes?

- How do young children learn; what do they need to know; and what curriculum is the most effective, efficient, and economical?

- What are the roles of women, especially mothers, in the family, the work force, and society?

- What are the roles and responsibilities of employers, religious institutions, and governments relating to the family?

IMPACT OF CURRENT
POLICIES ON ACCESS TO SERVICES

Mixed results characterize the federal and state efforts to fund and otherwise support ECEC services for children who need them while keeping in mind the governmental responsibility to meet the needs of those who most require support. The allocation of scarce resources, even for the categories of children who are served, continues to limit the availability of programs. Estimates for establishing enough ECEC programs for all children run to the billions of dollars. Federal requirements that Head Start and other ECEC programs collaborate in service delivery move slowly toward the goal of meeting the needs of all eligible children. Personal and societal growth and development resists change, even in the ECEC field, which can be, and often is, such a source of positive experiences to children and families.

Historically, the two streams from which today's ECEC programs developed—day nurseries in the field of social work and nursery schools and kindergartens in the field of education—have struggled with the American propensity to dichotomize, to resist federal interference in family life, and to emphasize the role of state and local governments in the lives of children. Children get caught among the mixed standards (NICHD Early Child Care Research Network, 1999). Examining the persistence of the dichotomy in another way may help.

Existing policies can be viewed in two ways: symbolic and tangible (Hy, 1978). Too often, *tangible policies* contained in the laws and regulations of a nation and its local entities are the primary focus of professionals and policy makers. An alternative viewpoint comes from the wealth of *symbolic policies* that are embedded regularly in the nooks and crannies of public action: in speeches, correspondence, legislative bills, and political appointments. If symbolic policies are tracked for potential impact on a field, leaders can build toward tangible action. The first six National Education Goals were crafted by President George H.W. Bush and the nation's 50 governors in 1989–1990. Those six and two others were enacted into law in the Goals 2000: Educate America Act of 1994. Goal One, on readiness, states that "by the year 2000, all children in America will start school ready to learn." Although that goal was not fully met by the year 2000, the statement itself has had an effect on federal, state, and local ECEC service policies. In the final analysis, tangible policies are made by the thoroughly democratic, frequently convoluted process of government that characterizes U.S. pluralistic society and political history. Change in such a political environment will continue to be slow, gradual, incremental, and marginal (Braybrooke & Lindblom, 1970).

In a democracy, advocates must work constantly to create positive change for the well-being of children and families. More dollars for more and improved services are sought with every legislative session. Beyond the promise of program expansion lies the reality born of collaboration, trade-offs, and achieving consensus. Although overtly focused on families on welfare or low-income working families, public ECEC policies can eventually benefit all families by setting the tone for quality that shapes programs and services in the ECEC field.

Even with erratic ECEC policies, programs for children continue to appear and the number of children enrolled in the programs continues to expand. The combination of the number of working mothers, single-parent families, and research findings about effective brain development in young children has struck a strong national nerve, and more policy makers are from a generation reared to expect women, even mothers, to be in the work force, and men, especially fathers, to invest in home life and child rearing.

Changes in the political and cultural perceptions of ECEC, although slow, gradual, incremental, and marginal, are occurring and must be recognized by ECEC leaders. For example, federal and state policies often encourage or require community-level collaboration among ECEC programs and the related family services of health, employment, housing, and transportation. In fact, in many states and localities, enterprising governors, innovative state legislators, and corporate leaders have joined with ECEC professionals, health providers, and parents from all socioeconomic levels to acknowledge and support the importance of early education and access to it; to value the nurturing of the future by small numbers of educated people; and to encourage and support the abilities of children to grow, develop, and take their places in the larger society.

REFERENCES

Adams, D., Foote, R.A., & Vinci, Y. (1996). *Making child care work: A study of child care resource and referral in the United States.* Washington, DC: National Association of Child Care Resource and Referral Agencies.

Adams, G., & Poersch, N.O. (1994). *Child care briefing packet*. Washington, DC: Children's Defense Fund.

Adams, G., & Poersch, N.O. (1996). *Who cares?: State commitment to child care and early education*. Washington, DC: Children's Defense Fund.

Bergmann, B.R. (1999, May). Making child care "affordable" in the United States. In S.W. Helburn (Ed.), The silent crisis in U.S. child care [Special issue]. *Annals of the American Academy of Political and Social Science, 563*, 208–219.

Bowman, B.T., Donovan, M.S., & Burns, M.S. (Eds.). (2001). *Eager to learn: Educating our preschoolers*. Washington, DC: National Academy Press.

Braybrooke, D., & Lindblom, C.E. (1970). *A strategy of decision: Policy evaluation as a social process*. New York: Macmillan.

Cahan, E.D. (1989). *Past caring: A history of U.S. preschool care and education for the poor, 1820–1965*. New York: National Center for Children in Poverty.

Capizzano, J., Adams, G., & Sonenstein, F.L. (2000, March). *Child care arrangements for children under five: Variations across states*. Washington, DC: Urban Institute Press.

Capiazzano, J., Adelman, S., & Stagner, M. (2002, June). *What happens when the school year is over?: The use and costs of child care for school-age children during the summer months* (Assessing the New Federalism, Occasional Paper Number 58). Washington, DC: Urban Institute.

Children's Defense Fund. (1999). *The state of America's children yearbook*. Washington, DC: Author.

Cost, Quality and Child Outcomes Study Team. (1995). *Cost, quality and child outcomes in child care centers*. Denver: Economics Department, University of Colorado at Denver.

Elementary and Secondary Education Act of 1965, PL 89-10, 20 U.S.C. §§ 241 *et seq.*

Final Rule–Head Start Program Performance Standards, 45 C.F.R. § 1304 (1996, November 5).

Gootman, J.A. (Ed.). (2000). *After-school programs to promote child and adolescent development: Summary of a workshop*. Washington, DC: National Academy Press.

Helburn, S.W. (Ed.). (1999, May). *The silent crisis in U.S. child care* [Special issue]. *The Annals of the American Academy of Political and Social Science, 563*.

Helburn, S.W., & Bergmann, B.R. (2002). *America's child care problem: The way out*. New York: Palgrave for St. Martin's Press.

Hy, R. (1978). Some aspects of symbolic education policy: A research note. *The Educational Forum, 42*(2), 203–209.

Individuals with Disabilities Education Act (IDEA) Amendments of 1997, PL 105-17, 20 U.S.C. §§ 1400 *et seq.*

Lake Research, Inc. (1996). *Report on child care focus groups*. Philadelphia & Kansas City, MO: The Pew Charitable Trusts & the Ewing Marion Kauffman Foundation.

Map to Inclusive Child Care Institute. (1999). *Conference program*. Washington, DC: U.S. Department of Health and Human Services, Administration for Children and Families, Administration for Children, Youth and Families, Child Care Bureau.

Marx, F., & Seligson, M. (1988). *The public school early childhood study: The state survey*. New York: Bank Street College of Education.

Morgan, G.G. (1998). *A hitchhiker's guide to the child care universe* (Rev. ed.). Washington, DC: National Association of Child Care Resource and Referral Agencies.

National Education Association. (1998, November). *Promoting quality in early care and education*. Washington, DC: Author.

NICHD Early Child Care Research Network. (1999, July). Child outcomes when child care center classes meet recommended standards for quality. *American Journal of Public Health, 89*(7), 1072–1077.

No Child Left Behind Act of 2001, PL 107-110, 20 U.S.C.

Román, J. (Ed.). (1998). *The NSACA standards for quality school-age care*. Boston: National School-Age Care Alliance.

Shonkoff, J.P., & Phillips, D.A. (Eds.). (2000). *From neurons to neighborhoods: The science of early childhood development*. Washington, DC: National Academy Press.

Smith, E.C. (n.d.). *Understanding child care supply and demand in the community: A workbook*. Chicago: The Enterprise Foundation.

Stebbins, H. (1998). *Improving services for children in working families*. Washington, DC: National Governors Association.

U.S. General Accounting Office. (1989, July). *Early childhood education: Information on costs and services at high-quality centers*. Washington, DC: Author.

U.S. General Accounting Office. (1998, January). *Welfare reform: States' efforts to expand child care programs*. Washington, DC: Author.

Whitebook, M., & Bellm, D. (1999). *Taking on turnover: An action guide for child care center teachers and directors*. Washington, DC: Center for the Child Care Workforce.

4

Regulatory Policy

Gwen G. Morgan

Governments can operate services, or they can leave such programs to be operated in the private market. Regulatory policy offers a third alternative: Governments can regulate programs that are operated in the private market. Regulatory policy enables governments to protect the public and to set a floor of quality for programs in the private sector. With regulation, it is not necessary or desirable to rely only on supply/demand to have a long-term effect on quality. Nor is government operation of services the only way to avert harm to children. Since the latter part of the 19th century, regulation, a peculiarly U.S. policy invention, has been a major factor, offering a middle alternative between big business and big government.

The first real licensing law for early childhood education and care (ECEC) in the United States was passed in Pennsylvania in the 1880s and was a precursor of strong regulatory reforms to come. By 1962, most states were licensing child care centers, and many were licensing family child care homes.

The general public supports some forms of regulation as a solution to public policy issues. Most of the public takes its regulatory environment for granted, voicing strong objection only when there is undue red tape or unreasonable rules. There have been, however, several waves of antiregulatory views. Following studies of large federal regulatory agencies in the 1970s and 1980s, many policy makers believed that regulatory agencies were captives of the industries they regulated, having lost their regulatory zeal in the process of identifying with the industry. This view still causes a reaction against the use of regulatory power to protect powerful interests, including powerful professions, but more recently it is usually directed against regulation of prices or entry into a field. Environmental protection and consumer protection are forms of regulation that have not lost their vitality and that retain their popularity in the political arena.

A more recent assault on regulation has been launched by policy makers who have fastened on to the idea of privatization and have suggested that it be applied to licensing. Actually, it is licensing and regulatory power that has made possible the success of privatizing certain services. For ECEC, for example, the majority of service for more than 100 years has been provided in the private sector and licensed by the government.

Although there has been some delegation of licensing by state licensing agencies to local public agencies, there has been little privatization of licensing. New Jersey experimented with privatizing the voluntary regulation of family child care but concluded after study that the effort had not been successful. As of 2002, there has been no serious effort at privatizing licensing of ECEC.

THE EXTENT OF REGULATION IN EARLY CHILDHOOD EDUCATION AND CARE

Each state has its own definition of what services it will license. In general, and with some major exceptions, the states license market programs, that is, programs that parents must seek outside the resources of the family and that are not provided through public entitlements or other federal programs (e.g., public education, Head Start). Some programs that are funded by the federal or state government may be regulated by funding requirements, even when they are not covered by licensing. Government-run programs are not required to be licensed because the public agency that runs them is responsible for their quality.

Market forms of care include the following:

- *Full-day centers:* These programs have various names, such as day nurseries, child development centers, early learning centers, and child care. Use of full-day programs has grown steadily since the

1980s. This growth may be due in part to the fact that many part-day programs began offering extended hour options to accommodate the needs of working parents during this period, as more and more mothers joined the work force. Twelve states exempt faith-based centers from licensing. A handful of states exempt Montessori schools.

- *Part-day nursery schools and preschools:* These programs are also market forms of care. They are, however, not licensed or regulated in 20 of the states.

- *Large and small family child care homes:* Care in the home of the provider of the care is called *family child care.* Large homes, or group family child care homes, are permitted to enroll a larger number of children, usually up to 12, with 2 caregivers. Many states have a threshold number of enrolled children that defines licensing, so a home with fewer than that number of children would not need to be licensed. Threshold numbers vary between 1 child in 14 states to 13 children in South Dakota. Three states do not license unsubsidized family child care. As a result, many small family child care homes are not licensed.

- *School-age programs:* School-age children may be enrolled in licensed centers or in licensed family child care homes. Another form of center, however, is the program exclusively for this age group, operating before and after school hours and during school vacations.

- *In-home care:* This type of care is the smallest segment of the ECEC field, provided in the child's home by nannies, au pairs, housekeepers, or baby sitters. Less than 6% of working parents use in-home care for children under 5. In-home care is market care that parents must find and employ, but it is not licensed. The assumption is that the care is provided by the caregiver as the employee of the parent rather than as a service holding itself out to the public.

Nonmarket care is not usually licensed. It includes the following:

- *Care by kith and kin:* Care by a parent at home or at work, care by a sibling, care by grandparents, and care by other relatives are all care by kin. *Kith* are very close friends of the family, who provide care for a specific child because of these close ties. States try to avoid regulating kith or kin, but have found it difficult to find a simple legal definition of kith.

LEVELS OF STANDARDS

It is useful to think of standards in the United States as defining different levels of quality. Licensing is the baseline of necessary quality that all programs must meet, which is set and enforced in each state. Programs can exceed this baseline, but they may not consistently fall below it. It is the minimum (meaning *at least* rather than *low*) that is required as essential to prevent harm. (Table 4.1 presents the different levels of standards in ECEC.)

If public funds are spent on the care provided, a higher level of quality can be expected, through funding standards. Still higher are standards for voluntary accreditation developed by private associations: by the National Association for the Education of Young Children (NAEYC) for centers, by the National Association for Family Child Care for family child care, and by the National School-Age Care Alliance for school-age programs.

Some states are offering to pay more for higher quality programs, often combining accreditation with funding specifications. Oklahoma has a one-, two-, and three-star rating system with differ-

Table 4.1. Levels of standards in early childhood education and care (ECEC), from lowest to highest

Type of standard	To whom applied	Legal powers used	Quality level
Licensing requirements	All market programs defined in law	Police powers	Quality must meet certain minimums.
Funding standards	All programs receiving certain public funds	Contractual agreement	Specifications for purchase must be met.
Accreditation standards	All who apply to be accredited	Voluntary agreement	High quality standards must be met.
Goal standards such as those set by the American Academy of Pediatrics	All who aspire to recommended practice, voluntarily	Used only as reference	Quality recommendations are based on expert advice.

ential reimbursement in a program called Reach for the Stars. North Carolina law requires that all licensees be rated between one star and five stars, using a rating scale to assess program quality rather than to give accreditation. In some counties, programs with five stars are paid a higher subsidy rate.

Many states, however, do not set higher standards than licensing for funded programs for eligible children because these states wish to avoid a segregating effect. Recently some states have begun to require accreditation by NAEYC as necessary for receiving public funds, such as when a state funds ECEC programs in public schools and wants some assurance of quality. This kind of mass accreditation requirement might strain the capability of the accrediting body.

In general, except in cases of child abuse or neglect, the states do not license care provided by parents, other relatives (kin), and very close family friends (kith), all of which are forms of care within the resources of the family and therefore are nonmarket forms. In addition, in most states, public schools are not regulated by licensing because they are the responsibility of a public agency, the state's education agency.

TRENDS TOWARD LOOSENING OR TIGHTENING REGULATION

Even though there is an antiregulatory climate in many states, the changes that states make to their licensing regulations generally tend to tighten the rules rather than loosen them. The most striking features about U.S. licensing policy are the fact of separate sets of regulations for each state and the striking differences that may exist between them. Some trends are evident in the changes in rules, including the following:

- More states are regulating group size in centers. In 1986, 31 states did not regulate group size for preschool children; however, in 1997, only 22 states did not regulate group size.

- Ratios for infants, preschool children, and school-age children have improved, but those for 2-year-olds have not. In 1986, 11 states set a child–adult ratio of 15:1 or higher for preschool children; but in

1997, only 4 states had that high a ratio. Infant–staff ratios also have become more stringent; the predominant ratio is 4:1.

- States have added substantial numbers of hours of ongoing training required for all staff, although preservice qualifications have not greatly improved.

RESPONSIBILITY FOR REGULATORY POLICY

ECEC regulatory policy is different for each of three major delivery systems: Head Start, the public schools, and the purchase-of-service system. Full-day Head Start is licensed by all of the states, and part-day Head Start is licensed in 30 states, unless it is a part of the public schools. In addition, programs must meet the higher set of standards (Final Rule–Head Start Program Performance Standards, 1996) required by the Head Start Bureau. The schools have very little regulation, other than a building code that is not designed with the education and development of young children in mind. Licensing does not apply to the public schools in most states. The state education agency may require schools to become privately accredited when they receive state and federal dollars. The ECEC centers and family child care homes in the purchase-of-service system are licensed by the licensing agency designated in the state's licensing law. The term *regulation* includes licensing and any other public, mandatory system of applying standards.

In the early 1960s, very few U.S. citizens expected that the government would not only regulate ECEC but would also begin to pay for it for large numbers of children. Many U.S. citizens see ECEC as a family responsibility (see Chapter 7), not a public responsibility, with support from government taking the form of regulation.

There is no federal form of licensing for ECEC. In general, the states are separately responsible for licensing, both for setting the rules and for ensuring that programs meet the rules. Agencies that deliver or fund services are responsible for fiscal monitoring. Licensing functions are defined in laws passed by the state legislatures.

Some states call their method of regulating *licensing,* and others call theirs *registration*. Neither term, however, relates to whether or how often the state visits the ECEC centers. Because Congress later made another definition for *registration,* to mean that states list the ECEC programs available but apply few or no standards, the use of the term *registration* is going to lead to great confusion. In general, most states that say they register are really using a method that meets a definition of licensing, that is, 1) standards are applied; 2) programs that meet the standards are permitted to operate; and 3) a license can be removed, or other sanctions applied, if a program does not meet the standards.

Most licensing laws include the following:

- A finding that child care is potentially hazardous

- A ban on providing ECEC when standards are not met

- Permission given to operate an ECEC program, but only to providers who are licensed by the state

- Right of the state licensing staff to enter and inspect the facility

- Advisory structures

- Enforcement methods (e.g., removal or suspension of license, fines)

- Delegation to the state licensing agency the task of writing licensing rules

- List of topics (e.g., qualifications of staff, safety of facilities and equipment, health procedures and equipment, discipline procedures, program of activities, staff ratios, group size, parent relations) for which rules may be written by the state licensing agency; if a topic is not mentioned on the statutory list, then the licensing agency cannot write rules to cover it

OTHER MECHANISMS FOR BASIC APPROVAL

The states usually require separate inspections from the public health system and from the building and fire safety systems, in addition to the inspection by the licensors. These are all baseline approvals, instituted in separate laws, in response to concerns about epidemic disease, building collapse, or catastrophic fires. States often have uniform sanitation codes, enforced by local public health officials, that apply to ECEC physical facilities and sanitary practices. States usually have either local building codes or a uniform state building code, enforced by a local building inspector, to protect against fire and building collapse. Some localities have additional fire safety codes applied locally through their fire departments. All of these local powers exerted by health and social services agencies and by planning boards are powers derived from state law. Local governments are created by the states.

In some states, the state law delegates licensing to local agencies that are permitted to write their own rules, so long as their rules are no less stringent than those set by the state. There is only one city, New York City, in which the local government has been able to write rules less stringent than those of its state. The city, however, does not have this authority for newer forms of regulated care, such as large or small family child care homes or school-age programs. The power to write its own rules has eroded in New York City.

Zoning is another form of regulation, used not for the purpose of protecting children and families but to protect property values. Local communities in most states are permitted to regulate land use through their state zoning laws, adding further to the complexity of regulation. A few states (e.g., California) prohibit local communities from using zoning powers to inhibit the growth of needed services.

The problems identified in the U.S. licensing system are not that rules are too stringent. Instead, licensees complain about the number of inspectors, the lack of system among them, and contradictory rules. In some geographical areas, particularly those with large cities, the number of inspectors and the separateness of their legal authority create a cumbersome situation in which getting licensed can take an entire year. Licensees complain that inspections are not done in a timely manner and that the rules of one agency are inconsistent with those of another, so to conform to one code is to be out of compliance with another code. Some localities have created a coordinating mechanism for inspections so that the program does not face conflicting rules or costly time delays.

THE STANDARDS DEVELOPMENT PROCESS

The development of standards within a state follows legal principles of representation of different parties affected by the standards (Jambor, 1964), in keeping with due process under the 14th Amendment to the U.S. Constitution. Typically, the licensing agency assembles a task force or an advisory group to write a particular set of standards. The different kinds of stakeholders in that service are represented: some experts and some parents. Their roles are to fully discuss and try to reach consensus on a new set of standards.

States change their rules when

- Their statutes require periodic review and change

- Changes in other states have resulted in their moving from a middle position in the states to a bottom position in terms of quality of care provided

- Outmoded standards that cause trouble for providers and do not have positive benefit to children have been identified for change

- New research findings no longer justify an existing rule or do justify changing a rule

- Changes in the field of practice have improved the level of quality to the point where providers support a change in rules

States need to justify their changes, and the most common rationales are common practice in other states and research findings.

After a process lasting close to a year, the standards development groups usually reach consensus, and the proposed new standards are brought before public hearings for comments. At this point, the lengthy process often proves to have been valuable because the advisory group or task force members can defend the proposed new standards if asked to.

To be enforced, the standards need the support of the centers and homes that are asked to meet them. If there is not a significant strong group of providers of care who are able and willing to meet the new standard, it cannot be enforced. The rules, however, are changed about every 3–5 years. Since the time they were last changed, the field of practice will have improved, influenced by such factors as training workshops and college courses, conferences, professional publication, accreditation, and goals standards.

Regulatory politics require some skill in uniting very different stakeholders in a common commitment, but the fact that standards regularly rise is evidence that this democratic process does result in change. It is the only process that can bring about a higher level of quality through licensing.

FOCUS OF REGULATION

ECEC standards are provider focused or facility focused or a combination of the two. Licensing standards are set in which the citizens of a state draw the line, defining the least acceptable level of care. ECEC licensing is, and should be, child focused, comprising a set of rights that children have in that state that meet a level of quality defined as necessary. Licensing is a consumer protection program, ensuring parents of safe choices.

The standards are facility focused in the legal sense. The license is granted to an individual responsible for a facility. A *facility* means a building, its surrounding land, its rooms, its equipment and supplies, its activities, its groupings, its staff, and its board of directors. Some have confused that legal sense with the narrower term *physical facilities,* which means only the place, building, and equipment. The standards are not facility focused in that narrower sense because they must include the qualifications of staff, the relationships and interactions among staff and children, and the activities that they and the children do. The attention in standards to the physical facility does not take the spotlight away from the staff, what they do, and what training they need to have.

Some states remain focused on the narrower definition of facilities because they associate licensing with the basic necessities, defined only as health and safety, and consider the program of activities and the relationships as having to do with child development, which these states regard not as a necessity, but as a luxury. Recent brain research makes focusing only on the basic necessities a badly outmoded idea. It is now known that children need relationships in order to stay alive, not just to learn and grow, and that serious harm can come to a child from a lack of relationships, just as from a nutritional lack, fire, or disease.

RATIONALE FOR LICENSING

The process of regulating the private sector mediates between supply and demand. Not all supply is acceptable. Some is determined to be potentially harmful, substandard, and unacceptable. The licensor's task is primarily to persuade, or secondarily to threaten, providers so that they will reach and maintain an acceptable level. Two extremes of regulation would be to make all of the supply inaccessible to parents unless it was of high quality or to allow any level of quality to exist if a parent might choose it. Licensing falls between the two.

The rationale for licensing is that it is essential to prevent harm to children. For any profession, a primary rule must be "First, do no harm." If the local, state, or federal government, however, is paying for a program, there is an additional rationale: to ensure effective use of public dollars. In this case, the funding agency wants to do more than prevent harm; it wants to get results for its public dollar. The rationale for accreditation has been to recognize a higher level of quality. If it is believed that higher quality is necessary in order to get results, then accreditation will be used in combination with funding levels.

ENFORCEMENT

State licensing statutes vary in the strength of their enforcement provisions. Enforcement is limited by due process rights of providers under the U.S. Constitution and the states' administrative procedures acts and strengthened by provisions in the licensing statute. In most states, enforcement strategies include

- Extending the time of provisional/probational license
- Restricting the terms of the license

- Changing license status from regular to provisional or probational
- Limiting expansion of the legal corporation
- Denying of a license
- Refusing to renew a license (only for cause)
- Suspending of license pending court hearing
- Obtaining a court-ordered injunction or suspension of license
- Revoking a license for cause
- Sending a notice of violation
- Sending a letter of warning

In addition to using these enforcement tools, licensors in some states can also

- Administer fines imposed by the licensing agency or ordered by a court
- Require licensees to take coursework
- Make extra visits to monitor the facility
- Post findings of licensing visits
- Make levels of compliance public
- Make ratings public
- Expand the licensing period for good compliance
- Use indicator checklists
- Monitor based on compliance records
- Streamline renewal or issue permanent licenses
- Use laptop computers for inspections
- Survey parents using the services provided by licensees

More sophisticated study is needed to identify differences among the states in the ways they implement the enforcement tools they have. States have difficulty in answering survey questions about numbers of visits or ECEC staff available because the question is much more complex than is realized.

Four potential indicators of effective enforcement may be difficult to determine because of missing data:

1. The number of sanctions permitted by statute to the licensing agency and whether and how often each is used.

2. The time between a visit that finds noncompliance and the next follow-up visit.

3. Number of centers closed down per every 100 licensees per year. These data should be the easiest to apply and to compare across the states. Failure to close down centers, however, might indicate failure to enforce the law, or it might mean diligence by the licensor in achieving compliance.

4. Number of licensors compared with number of licensable units. This data is easy to gather in states with state-operated licensing systems but not in states that use county staff as licensors.

Poor enforcement can be the result of a weak law that does not empower the licensing office to visit and make unannounced visits, that does not empower the licensing office to apply a variety of sanctions, and that inadequately delegates to the licensing office the capability to write and change licensing requirements. Poor enforcement could also be the result of inadequate training for licensing staff, such that they do not know how to enforce the law. Poor enforcement can also be the result of an antiregulatory political climate or a naïve assumption of a one-size-fits-all method of enforcement.

Licensors need to fit their methods to three very different types of providers of care. The first group is the "newcomers." For them, the requirements are an education in how to run their centers. They need help in finding ways to meet the requirements. The second group is the "forgetful licensees." They intend to meet the rules, but on any given day some other pressing issues cause them to forget the licensing rules for a time. That can happen so often that these licensees drift far from compliance with the rules. This is the largest group, by far. Confronted by serious emergencies, they need a reminder from the state that maintaining basic quality is a top priority. The third group is much smaller than the newcomers and the forgetful licensees. These few providers have no intention of meeting the rules.

They will try to keep their license without paying the cost of meeting the state's minimum standards. No amount of teaching or persuasion will change these providers. Flexibility prolongs the process forever. Only the potential loss of their license, or a substantial fine, will shape them up.

It is a very naïve climate of opinion that fosters the view that licensors should use the same tactics for each of these three types of provider. For all providers, licensors must abide by due process rights of citizens to be protected against inappropriate use of governmental power, but the licensors must also protect children's rights to a state-defined level of quality. These rights of children will clash with the providers' rights, but providers do not have the right to operate without meeting the level of quality required by the state.

THE LICENSING STAFF

Once the local approvals are gained for health and building safety, staff must be assigned from the licensing office to investigate new licensing applications, follow up on complaints, relicense, and educate the public. States create, organize, and reorganize their own regulatory agencies.

In some states, licensing is done by state staff, organized into regional offices. With this arrangement, the state has maximum control and has the greatest chance of achieving a uniform statewide level of quality. Family child care is most often regulated by social services agency staff at the county level, who are also responsible for recruiting needed services and who answer to the local commissioners, not the state licensing office. States with such arrangements have difficulty estimating caseloads because it is not clear which county staff are assigned to licensing.

Most of these staffing patterns involve delegation of state licensing to public local agencies. Some state laws delegate licensing powers or permit such delegation to local public agencies. For example, in Massachusetts, an old law permitted the state to delegate licensing to local boards of health, provided that they used the same standards and assigned adequate staff to the task. This state has found that the local cities are returning licensing to the state, not wishing to take on liability locally.

There is very little delegation of licensing to private organizations. In New Jersey, where licensing is voluntary for family child care home providers, the state made a concerted effort to delegate family child care regulation to private resource and referral agencies at the local level, but the experiment was not judged a success. The cost was high, state ability to control quality was limited, and the local agencies found that the licensing function inhibited their ability to deliver resource and referral services.

Until recently, most states reported that they were not adequately staffed for licensing an expanding set of ECEC services. Well-staffed licensing offices facilitate the growth of new supply, but understaffing creates bottlenecks and barriers to supply of ECEC. In part, understaffing has been a problem plaguing ECEC licensing in many states from its beginnings. Very little data has been available from the states on their caseloads, primarily because states have inadequate information on local county licensing for family child care. Data exists on how many centers and family child care homes states have licensed, but as stated previously, only weak data on their staffing are available. Since the late 1990s, however, in response to welfare reform, many more states have expanded their licensing staffs for ECEC. Oklahoma and Illinois, for example, added substantial new staff in 1998–1999.

Licensing staff are covered by civil service preferential provisions, which means that in many states a less qualified person can be given the job ahead of a more qualified one, if the person getting the job is a veteran of civil service. Leaving that problem aside, it does not appear that the states have established the appropriate civil service qualifications for licensing in the first place. For example, in Massachusetts, the civil service test is about child psychology, which is not at all a good fit for what a licensor needs to know.

A more fitting civil service test would require knowledge of child development, of recommended practices in centers and family child care homes, of parents and culture, and of the basics of law enforcement and some strong experience in operating ECEC programs, particularly of the type the licensor is going to inspect. The National Association for Regulatory Administration has developed a training program for licensors (Gazan & Stevens, 1989). Groups of licensors who are members of NAEYC have been working on a recommended civil service test for licensors. Only Michigan requires its licensing staff to have a master's degree in early childhood education, social work, or child development with 2 years of professional experience.

MECHANISMS FOR
PROVIDING CONSUMER INFORMATION

As stated previously, licensing is a consumer protection form of regulation, and its standards represent legal rights that children have. Most states, however, initially added ECEC licensing to their child welfare services, such as foster care, in which children were likely to be without parents to speak for them. Parents used the licensing office to help them find ECEC and to report harm, but the role of parents was not at first designed to be a strong one. From the 1960s to the 1980s, the state licensing offices were the primary source of either consumer information or provider information. During that time, ECEC services expanded significantly in response to new legislation providing federal funding (e.g., Head Start, Social Services Block Grant, Temporary Assistance for Needy Families [TANF]). Few colleges were teaching ECEC, and only a handful of resource and referral agencies existed nationwide. The licensing offices were still the best source of information for both consumers and providers at that time. By the 1990s, many additional sources of information were available both for parents and for providers: the colleges, consultants, and the resource and referral system.

Child care resource and referral (CCR&R) agencies began in 1972, in Cambridge, Massachusetts; San Francisco and Oakland, California; and Rochester, Minnesota. Since that time, they have grown to become a nationwide network and a stronger voice for parents than the licensing offices alone. Both the licensing offices and the CCR&R agencies have, however, been timid about giving parents specific information about programs. The licensing offices have concentrated on improving the programs, and the CCR&R agencies have concentrated on helping parents make expert choices.

Parents calling a CCR&R agency or a licensor typically ask for a list and want to know which programs are trustworthy. They ask, "Would you put your child in that program?" The licensing office's response is usually a list, whereas the CCR&R agency's response is usually a handbook or extensive telephone coaching on how to choose. Both groups have been avoiding potential liability rather than designing information systems that are reasonable and helpful to consumers. Liability, however, is not incurred when correct factual information is shared. Both groups have overestimated parents' ability to make wise choices and to see potentially harmful conditions on their own, without specific consumer information. The Cost, Quality and Child Outcomes Study Team (1995) found that parents have very similar wishes for child care compared with those of experts but that parents are less able to recognize at a glance whether a program has those qualities or not. In general, most consumers of any product need concrete information or even ratings to help them.

One legal problem has caused much withholding of information from parents. When a program is being investigated in response to a complaint about a licensing violation or an instance of abuse or neglect in ECEC and the results of that investigation are not yet known, the licensing agency usually withholds the fact of the investigation both from parents and from CCR&R agencies. It is obvious that the agency cannot release the results of the investigation until it is completed, but when much time elapses between the complaint and the finding, both the CCR&R agency and the licensing agency are at risk of harming children by withholding the fact that an investigation is taking place. It is hard to imagine that the public and the courts would consider the withholding of this information reasonable if another child were to be seriously harmed in the interim.

The trend in the United States since the late 1990s has been to make more information available to parents. The licensing record, except for unsubstantiated complaints, is now accessible to parents and to CCR&R agencies. Parents need help in from licensing offices and from CCR&R agencies in interpreting these records and distinguishing complaints from noncompliance. The list of licensed programs is or will be available on the Internet in most areas. More emphasis on rating and specific information about the available programs is only beginning to be made.

A few new examples of provision of consumer information are the following:

- The CCR&R agency in Madison, Wisconsin, has rated every center in its county on its licensing record and has made the rating available to parents.

- As stated previously, the state of North Carolina has passed a law requiring the licensing office to rate each licensee with between one and five stars. Each center must receive a rating of at least one star; higher ratings are given for higher quality care. Ratings are to be based on a rating scale for ECEC such as the Early Childhood Environment Rating Scale–Revised Edition (Harms, Clifford, & Cryer, 1998) or the Infant/Toddler Environment Rating Scale (Harms, Cryer, & Clifford, 1990).

- Sixteen states are paying a higher per-child rate to accredited programs. Parents in those states can get information from the CCR&R agencies about whether a program is operating at the minimum level established for licensing and whether it is accredited and, in some states, whether it is at another level between these two.

NONLICENSING
APPROACHES TO IMPROVING QUALITY

Regulatory tools for improving quality include required professional training and credentials; licensing of individuals; funding standards; differential reimbursement rates based on quality; and mandated credentials.

Licensing is only one of the many tools that states and advocates can use to bring about ECEC quality. A wide variety of quality initiatives have been expanding rapidly recently, using federal money from the TANF and Child Care and Development Fund (CCDF; discussed in Chapters 1 and 3) programs. To encourage the growth of ECEC program quality, a credential for program directors is under development in many states. Most likely it will eventually be tied to funding standards or to licensing. Tiered reimbursement rates (i.e., paying higher subsidies for higher quality ECEC) have spread to 16 states since 1992 and are under consideration in others. A practitioner registry, public or private, to track the qualifications of staff, is required by law in Wisconsin and is being developed in other states (e.g., Connecticut, Delaware, Massachusetts).

In many states, there is strong interest in ensuring that licensing is consistent with the career development approach to staffing, salaries, and job mobility. The U.S. Department of Labor is expanding apprenticeship programs to the ECEC field in half of the states, and at least 10 states have adopted the T.E.A.C.H. (Teacher Education and Compensation Helps) Early Childhood scholarship program to enable staff to reach higher levels of college preparation. Many of these innovations are based in the agencies that also license.

Some of the factors that might be built into licensing that will help career development are

- Allowing the director credential to be one of the ways of meeting director qualifications
- Listing levels of roles (e.g., teacher and lead teacher)
- Providing multiple alternatives in qualifications
- Specifying training content and requiring distribution of topics
- Incorporating agreed-on competencies for practitioners into content requirements
- Providing licensure of individuals
- Offering a registry for practitioners
- Encouraging involvement of licensing staff in career development planning

It is important to remember that different forms of regulation exist, and other nonregulatory ways of raising quality are available. Although licensing establishes the baseline of acceptable quality, states have many other strategies to help programs achieve levels of quality higher than what is required. Nonregulatory tools for improving quality are professional training, consumer information and ratings, newsletters and other publications, accreditation, credentialing of staff, and resource and referral functions.

RELATIONSHIP BETWEEN REGULATORY POLICY FOR EARLY CHILDHOOD EDUCATION AND CARE AND REGULATORY POLICY FOR OTHER SOCIAL SERVICES

Social services and educational services are regulated by the states in the United States. With other services, the state may have other powers, in addition to the police powers on which licensing is based, with which to encourage compliance with its standards. The state is using governmental powers used to establish policy for the level of quality for all children that is acceptable in the state.

For other services, whether or not licensed, government has other more powerful policy tools, such as the power of mandatory standards for insurance, the power to place children in the care of the state, or the power of contract law to implement a funding agreement, to set a floor of quality. For example, there is additional power available to the states in the realm of child welfare services. Here, the states often have placement powers and control over the child. They can use their placement powers to demand quality much more easily than they could use their licensing power, even though the services are also licensed. The placement powers enable the states to set their licensing rules at a higher level because the providers of foster care do not have the strong due process rights that licensees have under the law. This mechanism of quality improvement, however, does not reach the total population of children in need of foster care.

For ECEC, the state can use its contract agreements with providers to get them to agree to provide a higher level of quality, but that is limited to affecting subsidized children. A large number of children who are enrolled in ECEC programs are not eligible for any governmental subsidy. The state's power to use contract law to improve quality affects some eligible children, but it is the basic licensing rules alone that protect all children. There is a large "gap group" of two-parent working families whose combined earnings are too high for them to receive help with their ECEC but too low to pay the cost of quality ECEC. The lack of societal supports to this group has kept U.S. ECEC quality poor to mediocre and the salaries of its providers low.

REFERENCES

Cost, Quality and Child Outcomes Study Team. (1995). *Cost, quality, and child outcomes in child care centers.* Denver: University of Colorado, Center for Research in Economics and Social Policy, Department of Economics.

Final Rule–Head Start Program Performance Standards, 45 C.F.R. § 1304 (1996, November 5).

Gazan, H.S., & Stevens, C. (1989). Licensing enforcement. In *NARA licensing curriculum* (Chapter 4). St. Paul, MN: National Association for Regulatory Administration.

Gormley, W.T., Jr. (1998, June). Regulatory enforcement styles. *Political Research Quarterly, 51*(2), 363–383.

Harms, T., Clifford, R.M., & Cryer, D. (1998). *Early Childhood Environment Rating Scale–Revised Edition.* New York: Teachers College Press.

Harms, T., Cryer, D., & Clifford, R.M. (1990). *Infant/Toddler Environment Rating Scale.* New York: Teachers College Press.

Jambor, H.A. (1964). Theory and practice in agency participation in the formulation of child care licensing standards. *Child Welfare, 63,* 521–528.

Morgan, G. (1989). *Summary report on state delegation of licensing to local agencies: Study conducted for state of Maryland.*

Morgan, G. (1996). *The facts of life: How child care licensing requirements are created.* Boston: Center for Career Development in Early Care and Education.

5

Staff Roles, Education, and Compensation

Gwen G. Morgan

In the United States, there is no single system for setting qualifications for early childhood workers because there is not a single system for delivering early childhood education and care (ECEC) to children. Instead, there are three major systems and a few smaller ones. The three major systems are

1. Head Start, serving very low-income preschool children and infants/toddlers, of whom 10% have special needs

2. The purchase-of-service system, serving preschool children, infants/toddlers, and school-age children outside of school hours, part- and full-time in private centers and homes

3. The public school system, offering education for children of mandatory school-age and sometimes preschool programs and programs outside of school hours

Each of these systems has its own supportive infrastructure—its own standards, history, training, research, concepts and myths, and leaders and constituencies. Each has its own staff roles and its own names for these roles.

STAFF ROLES AND CHARACTERISTICS

The Bureau of Labor Statistics Occupational Employment Survey (OES) Report (1996) has two job classifications for the person in charge of a group of children in a child care center. One, "child care worker," is a classification of those who dress, bathe, feed, and supervise play, a description that would fit the role of assistant teacher. A second role identified in the OES Report is "preschool teacher." This role is classified among professional occupations and is defined as one who instructs children in a preschool program or child care center. It appears that if a staff person is responsible for the educational program, conceptualized as instruction, that person is a preschool teacher, not a worker.

As an occupational group, ECEC workers are relatively well educated. In the Cost, Quality and Child Outcomes (CQO) Study, center teachers (including lead teachers) had an average of 2 years of college (CQO Study Team, 1995). Assistant teachers averaged almost 1 year of postsecondary education. Thirty-one percent of center staff had college degrees, a little more than the percentage of all service workers with college degrees (CQO Study Team, 1995).

In the field of practice, those working in the purchase-of-service system for young children in licensed centers have a wide mix of credentials. A few have master's degrees. More have bachelor's degrees. Still more have associate's degrees or the Child Development Associate (CDA) credential. A large number have no degrees.

The role of these individuals is conceptualized differently in the three different systems. Head Start and the purchase-of-service system vary widely but are likely to view the role as specialized for young children and also more likely to view parent relations as central to the work. The schools are most likely to view the role as school teacher.

To some degree, these differing attitudes are reinforced by the colleges. Accessible college training for ECEC workers with a focus on children from birth to 5 years old is most likely to be found in the community college system and a few private colleges (Morgan et al., 1993). Most of the 4-year institutions offering courses of study on ECEC are public colleges that offer training geared to the public school teacher certification requirements. Out of necessity, these college programs emphasize teaching skills for kindergarten through third grade rather than emphasize the younger age groups or the needs of school-age children outside of school hours.

State licensing rules and their rationale have also influenced individuals' attitudes toward their work. In many states, a child development program is clearly described in the rules. In those states, a "custodial" program, in which children's basic health and safety needs are met without activities focusing on children's development and education, is illegal.

The ECEC work force in the United States is 97% female. Most would prefer a more gender-mixed work force, and center directors were having some success in attracting more men to the field in the mid-1980s. The effort was derailed, however, by a public hysteria about alleged sexual abuse of children in ECEC centers. The effect of that period is still with us. Caregivers, even women, are not trusted to touch children or give them love. It takes an unusually self-confident man to enjoy the work when surrounded with such distrust. The higher education system might be able to help with this through strategic placement and supervision of male students in programs, offering support to both the male student and the center.

As U.S. children in ECEC programs become more diverse, the work force for children's programs must reflect this diversity so that children can have hope for their own futures (Washington & Andrews, 1998). Data from the Boston Early Education Quality Improvement Project (1997) indicated that family child care providers match the children they serve in ethnic and linguistic background. School-age child care programs are more diversely staffed than ECEC centers are, and centers are more diverse than public schools. By far, the least diversity is found among public school teachers.

STAFF QUALIFICATIONS

In the United States, there is not a single coherent system of staff qualifications. Each state develops its own teacher credential, and each state writes its own licensing qualifications. The federal government administers Head Start and sets its standards.

The "Big Picture" chart (see Table 5.1) maps a few of the major roles in the three systems, a few others in early intervention, and some significant roles in the infrastructure for one state. It is intended

Table 5.1. The "Big Picture" chart: Qualifications for roles in early care and education in one state

Academic levels (or the equivalent)	Child care centers and infant/toddler programs	Head Start programs	Family child care homes	School-age child care programs	Hospitals	Early intervention programs	Child care resource and referral (CCR&R) agencies	Public schools
Doctorate								
National Early Childhood Certification								
Master's degree	Lead teacher, alternative 6							Principal
State departments of education Early Childhood Certification	Lead teacher, alternative 5				Specialists	Specialists		Program director; Teacher
Bachelor's degree	Lead teacher, alternative 4; Director II						CCR&R director	Provisional teacher
Child Life Credential					Child life play specialist			
Associate's degree	Lead teacher, alternative 3; Director I	Director II; Director I				Director		Even Start (Assistant teacher)
Department of Labor (DOL) Child Development Specialist credential	Lead teacher, alternative 2	Parent coordinator		Director				
Child Development Associate	Lead teacher, alternative 1	Teacher						
Four courses								
Department of Public Health certification of Infant/Toddler Specialist				School-age child care site coordinator; School-age child care kindergarten coordinator		Infant/toddler caregiver; Early intervention home visitor		
One course	Teacher	Home visitor	Competent family child care provider	School-age child care group leader			CCR&R parent counselor	
Orientation	Assistant teacher	Assistant teacher	Family child care provider	Assistant teacher				
Aide	Aide	Aide		Aide				

as a conceptual overview, not as a complete picture of the rich array of roles that exist in the field of ECEC. It is also possible to use this type of chart as a guide to thinking about roles that might be missing or underdeveloped. For example, although the teacher role is emphasized in public education, there are seldom requirements regarding or training offered to assistant teachers or aides. There is therefore a lot of blank space in the public school column of Table 5.1 in the roles prior to the teacher role.

On the other hand, in family child care, there are no identified high-level roles requiring rigorous preparation. This field has more white at the top of the column in the figure and needs to develop some higher level roles and pathways to these roles (e.g., training specialist, home visitors, mentor provider, system director).

Licensing, as described in Chapter 4, does not usually apply to the public schools and often does not apply to Head Start. Although there are many examples of successful partnerships and efforts to collaborate to bring about a single ECEC system with greater coherence, these three systems remain largely unconnected at both the program and the policy levels.

Head Start Qualifications

Head Start relies heavily on funding standards called the Head Start Performance Standards (Final Rule–Head Start Program Performance Standards, 1996) for achieving quality. Head Start employs teachers, parent specialists, health coordinators, and workers in a variety of other roles. It did not initially stress college credits in its credentialing as the schools have done. When it began in 1965, it did not require degrees in education or social work. Consistent with its philosophy of empowering parents and members of a child's community, it initially avoided rigorous academic expectations while maintaining high expectations for comprehensive service through its standards.

The CDA credential, a national competency-based credential, was developed in 1971 for Head Start workers as an alternative to the rigidity that Head Start found in the world of higher education. It is administered by the Council for Professional Recognition, which has granted more than 100,000 credentials for Head Start employees, as well as center staff and family child care providers. It established a pragmatic goal of having at least one CDA in every classroom and has been nearing national success in this goal. Little by little, the CDA has become known and accessible to licensed centers and family child care. It is now written into 48 states' licensing requirements as one alternative way of qualifying for a role in providing ECEC. States value the CDA in various way: Hawaii established the CDA as qualifying staff to become teacher aides, and in 18 other states, the CDA qualifies a person to direct a center.

The CDA has also become more closely tied to college training. Recently, Congress enacted into law a requirement that 50% of Head Start classroom staff have associate or bachelor's degrees by 2003. This new mandate makes it important for the CDA credential to easily lead to a college degree.

Public School System Qualifications

The public school system does not have Head Start's faith in performance standards as the route to quality. In fact, a major problem in public education that interferes with quality has been the rigidity of its procedural rules, removing autonomy from the teaching staff and principals. People involved in public education do not automatically have the positive attitude toward input standards that Head Start people do. Most schools must meet few if any programmatic standards, other than a mandate to offer school for 180 days every year. A push toward school reform, however, has brought with it a strong belief in measuring results. If the child is viewed as the product of the schools, then how well children perform on tests is a measure of teacher competence.

The public school system and its unions and the state agencies responsible for education have over the years built a teacher license in each state (formerly called a teaching certificate) that is based on at least a bachelor's degree, and often a master's degree, specialized for education. In contrast, college degrees and teacher certification is generally not necessary to qualify a teacher to work in private schools, Head Start, or the purchase-of-service system. The emphasis of the entire system is on the role of teacher. There are seldom any qualifications required for teacher aides, who are not usually expected to become teachers. In some states, teacher certification is not required to qualify a teacher to teach young children in a public school. In those states, however, the schools may hire early childhood teachers at a lower rate of pay when they are not certified.

In many states, there is strong interest among some educators and advocates in delivering ECEC to 3- and 4-year-olds in part-day programs run by public schools. Some states, such as Texas, have begun to support programs for children from low-income families or low-income areas, using state money and Title I of the Elementary and Secondary School Act of 1965 (PL 89-10) and its amendments. Some states (e.g., Connecticut, Georgia, New Jersey, New York, Oklahoma) have made a start on universal prekindergarten education, sometimes contracting services from private ECEC programs in addition to operating programs directly. Very few states' teacher certifications, however, require teachers to have a practicum with children younger than kindergarten age when they are certified to work with this younger age group.

Purchase-of-Service System Qualifications

The purchase-of-service system, the third major early childhood delivery system, is a stream of federal and state dollars that permits the state to buy in, for eligible children, to licensed private centers and large and small family child care homes that serve the general population. Some states contract for services for a specified number of spaces, whereas others contract for a single child through a voucher. Many do both. Much of the federal money appropriated for ECEC is spent by social services agencies either in purchase-of-service contracts for a specified number of spaces, or vouchers for specific children. Licensing sets standards for the ECEC *facility,* which means the building and grounds, all of the indoor and outdoor equipment and supplies, all of the staff, the program, all of the activities, and the governance (see Chapter 4 for further discussion of the term *facility*). For this system, staff qualifications are therefore set in facility standards. The licensing rules establish the required qualifications for identified roles. Only 12 states establish a lead teacher role, a job classification requiring higher qualifications. In those states, teachers are motivated to take more college courses to qualify to teach in this more responsible and better-paying role.

Three different kinds of training may be required in the licensing rules: 1) preservice training, 2) annual hours of ongoing training, or 3) basic orientation. When preservice training is required for a certain staff role, the individual must complete the training before being employed in the role. Annual ongoing training is a continuing requirement every year that a staff person must complete a certain number of hours of new training. This training is not required to be credit-bearing. Basic orientation training is usually brief and is required after an individual is hired but before the person assumes full responsibility of the role.

In several states the licensing agency centralizes the monitoring of staff qualifications by establishing a registry of staff (e.g., Connecticut, Delaware, Massachusetts, Wisconsin). At least one of the states (i.e., Massachusetts) issues a license to qualified individuals, which signifies that they have had a certain level of training that qualifies them for a particular role. These states are using their facility licensing rules to issue portable licenses to individuals as well as to facilities.

In some states, the preservice requirements for staff in centers and homes are very low or even nonexistent. They vary from two preservice college courses required in Illinois to no training at all required in Michigan. It has proved politically difficult for the states to raise the preservice qualifications since the 1980s. In part, the anti-regulatory climate has made policy makers unwilling to empower a profession to keep others out. A portion of the difficulty stems from the potential effect on costs to the general public, because licensed programs are not subsidized for all of the families who cannot afford them.

Even though standards for preservice qualifications have not changed much since the 1980s, there has been a very strong trend to add annual ongoing training requirements. Most states now have a requirement that all staff have a certain number of hours of training each year. In some cases, this ongoing training requirement is substantial enough that it could be used over time to meet the preservice requirements for the next higher role, if such training is available for credit and affordable.

USE OF CONTINUING EDUCATION

The use of continuing education differs in the three main ECEC systems. A major difference is the fact that in public education, as in traditional professions, the staff member already has an advanced degree. For many roles in ECEC, the people on the professional path do not yet have a degree. For these people, the continuing education is not only a way of deepening their knowledge for the roles they are in but also a way of qualifying themselves for later roles.

Head Start and some ECEC programs are using the national CDA credential, which requires substantial hours of continuing education units or one course as part of its renewal process. In these instances, the CDA-qualified individual usually does not yet have a 4-year degree or even, in some cases, a 2-year degree. Setting stringent national guidelines for its continuing education units (CEUs), Head Start is making this renewal process an incentive to pursue a degree, especially now that Head Start has a mandate to employ degreed staff in its classrooms. The national CEU standards require that 10 clock hours of training occur for each CEU, that the training be given by a qualified trainer, and that evidence of learning be provided in the form of a product from the participant.

The CDA usually represents about half of a 2-year degree. Some community colleges have begun to design a 2-year degree that applies the CDA as 9–12 credits toward an associate's degree. The CDA is not treated as a terminal degree; indeed, there is no terminal degree in a lifelong learning process. This concept of *professional development* or *career development* is one that fits the ideals of the field better than concept of becoming a paraprofessional because the teaching staff are all on a professional path, with no required stopping places, and no class distinctions.

This emerging pathway concept is by no means accepted by all factions in the field. Some strongly believe that the CDA should be the professional role that defines the field. There are equally strong believers in the associate's degree and equally strong believers in the bachelor's and master's degrees as defining the field. Many professionals in the field are caught between 19th-century credentialist views of professionalism and a more modern and more mobile approach. Two important initiatives in the field can be seen as integrating what might have been paraprofessional training with professionalism.

The Department of Labor's (DOL) apprenticeship program in ECEC results in a Child Development Specialist credential. In West Virginia, for example, a person in this program is employed (usually as an aide or assistant) while an apprentice, working extensively under supervision and taking two semesters of college courses in child development. At the end of this apprenticeship, the participant receives college credit for the work and becomes a Child Development Specialist. The training is approved as meeting standards for CDA training. When the individual attains this status, the program where the apprentice has worked employs the person and increases her or his wages. By prearrangement, the college credit earned can be applied to a degree program when the individual wishes to increase qualifications. Currently, DOL is expanding this program nationally. The Child Development Specialist is not stuck at a paraprofessional level. The apprentice training is accepted in degree-granting colleges, and there are no limits on what roles the specialist may pursue. DOL has adopted a more modern, more dynamic concept of professional training.

The T.E.A.C.H. (Teacher Education and Compensation Helps) Early Childhood Project has many similar goals to the DOL apprenticeship. T.E.A.C.H. began in North Carolina and has spread to six other states with the help of employer dollars (Colorado, Florida, Georgia, Illinois, Pennsylvania, Wisconsin). It is a scholarship program geared to individuals already working in ECEC centers or homes. Funds come from federal, state, and private sources. The director of the program agrees to release time so that participants can attend college courses and sometimes pays for the books or other expenses. The participant agrees to stay at the same ECEC program for a year after completing her or his T.E.A.C.H. educational goals. The director agrees to pay the participant a higher salary or a bonus when the goal is completed. The T.E.A.C.H. program pays for the college courses. The courses may also be subsidized by the state, as in the case of community college courses. The academic goals are set by the participant, who may later set higher goals and enter the program again. This scholarship program can be used for entry-level training for assistants or for graduate degrees for teachers or directors. Similar to the DOL apprenticeship program, T.E.A.C.H. has a concept of continued further education and lateral or vertical job mobility tied to college courses and degrees.

TRAINING FOR FAMILY CHILD CARE PROVIDERS

Training was seldom required in family child care until relatively recently. During the 1980s and 1990s, a large number of states added a requirement of ongoing hours of annual training for family child care, for both large homes and small homes. During the 1990s, more family child care providers have had access to CDA training and the CDA credential. In addition, a new accreditation has been developed by the National Association for Family Child Care (NAFCC) and is now emerging from its pilot phase. Because family child care quality is so closely related to the caregiver's knowledge and skills, the accreditation is often thought of as a credential. Even though accreditation sets standards for facilities as a whole, it also serves to train caregivers in the competencies they need. Family caregivers with the CDA are given credit for meeting some of the NAFCC accreditation criteria.

FUNDING OF CONTINUING EDUCATION

Various sources of funding support continuing education. Often, training is not subsidized at all, and small centers pay for training their own staff out of their ECEC income from parent fees. Once trained, this staff often leaves for higher paying jobs in schools, employer centers, or upscale chains. These small centers cannot afford to bear the training burden for the entire system.

A significant number of public dollars have been spent in training. Many of the states fund their child care resource and referral (CCR&R) agencies to provide training for family child care and center staff. Much of the noncredit training is offered by the CCR&R network. The T.E.A.C.H. Early Childhood and DOL apprenticeship programs have been funded by a variety of sources, including employers, foundations, and the public sector. The CDA program has scholarship money available to Head Start, centers, and homes, under federal CDA legislation. Federal financial aid is not yet geared to the needed expansion of the ECEC work force. ECEC staff, earning poverty wages, qualify for federal aid, but Pell grants are not available for one course at a time, the way most low-income employed individuals need them. Pell grant recipients must be at least half-time matriculated students in higher education.

CONTENT OF PROFESSIONAL TRAINING

There are varied models for the content of professional training, most of which have similar topics and information but are delivered under varied formats, with differing details in the information included. The CDA credential, for example, has identified six competency areas for teachers to include in their practice. In general, these are the basic areas that are taught at different levels as competencies develop and are deepened by further education. Many community colleges have based their associate's degree on the CDA competencies and, as stated previously, often give credit for CDA training and for the CDA in a certificate program that counts toward the associate's degree.

In some states (e.g., Connecticut, New York, Washington State), advocates for professional development have identified and reached statewide consensus on core knowledge or core competencies. Those that did this found it useful for articulating programs from one college level to the next and for reaching articulation agreements so that individuals' prior educational experiences can count toward degrees.

Much more study is needed of the content of training offered in the ECEC field. A baseline study, *Making a Career of It: The State of the States Report on Career Development in Early Care and Education* (Morgan et al., 1993), identified some initial gaps, but its scope did not include the detail that is now needed. At the time of that study, little advanced training was offered to family child care providers. One state actually required providers to repeat their entry-level training at the end of 3 years. There was almost no training to work with infants/toddlers or to work with school-age children outside of school hours. There was not enough training in how to include children with special needs and how to overcome biases among other parents and teachers against their inclusion. There was limited training on diversity issues.

A large unmet training need for directors of centers was found by this study. Little preparation existed for management roles in 1992. Since that baseline study, a number of communities/states have embarked on developing a credential for directors, typically requiring training in child development, family development, budget and fiscal reporting, personnel management and human relations, and internal and external policy. Several of these locally initiated projects have already graduated more than 100 credentialed directors. In Mississippi, the director credential is offered in noncredit training, and in Wisconsin, six college courses are required. A national project called Taking the Lead: Investing in Early Childhood Leadership for the 21st Century is stimulating director credentialing and leadership development.

In some states, the educational agency has emphasized training about children with special needs in the teacher credential, either by creating a specialized credential for teaching children with special needs or by building in requirements that all teachers must have skill in teaching special needs children.

Content in diversity also needs to be strengthened. The children of tomorrow in the United States will not be predominantly Caucasian. In the near future, the majority of Americans will be from a mosaic of ethnic and racial backgrounds (Washington & Andrews, 1998). There is less emphasis on diversity as a content area in the preparation of school teachers than for staff in Head Start or the purchase-of-service system. Diversity is a part of accreditation standards and is in the licensing rules in a few states. In one state, Minnesota, every teacher in a licensed program must have taken a course in cultural dynamics. The entire area of training that prepares staff to work with increasingly diverse populations has not been studied. Anecdotal evidence, from career development and training work in most states, suggests that those states with greatest diversity (e.g., California, Florida, New York, Texas) are leaders in terms of their training, whereas most others lag far behind.

The importance of engaging parents and supporting families, so valued in Head Start, is not emphasized in depth in most teacher preparation programs. The Council for Professional Recognition has developed a CDA certificate for home visitors, a role often neglected in licensing. Head Start uses home visitors for parenting education and family support. A few states' health departments, responsible for children from birth to 3 years old with special needs, have developed their own credential for the early childhood classroom role. The roles in CCR&R are not required to be licensed in any state except Kansas, and training is largely nonexistent for CCR&R directors, telephone counselors, provider trainers and recruiters, and family child care home visitors.

COMPENSATION FOR STAFF

The Bureau of Labor Statistics provides data on 764 occupations in its OES Report, in an effort to simplify occupational titles consistently across agencies and auspices. Only 15 jobs have lower median wages than child care workers (Bureau of Labor Statistics, 1996).

As described previously, two different job roles are actually defined in the OES Report, which do not completely fit the roles as they exist in the field. The first, "child care workers," earned $6.12 per hour in 1996. The other role, "preschool teacher," is classified among professional occupations. This group earned a median income of $7.80 (Bureau of Labor Statistics, 1996). These figures are very close to the mean wages earned in 1993 by teachers and assistants in the CQO Study, $7.22 and $5.70, respectively (CQO Study Team, 1995).

Studies (Whitebook, Howes, & Phillips, 1998) reveal that assistants earn low wages ($6–$7 an hour), and that teachers are paid $7.36–$12.27 per hour, across all auspices. No studies have been done to find whether teachers with higher degrees earn more money than those without such degrees. Nor do we know whether the current labor shortage is resulting in higher pay for those with higher qualifications.

Less than half of center teaching staff in the purchase-of-service system have fully covered health insurance for themselves, and only 16% of those with full coverage received fully paid coverage for their dependents.

Teachers who work in the public school system teaching children in grades K–12 must meet teacher certification requirements, which vary from state to state. These teachers receive better pay than teachers in Head Start or the purchase-of-service ECEC system and are qualified by college degrees. In many localities they earn roughly twice what a teacher in ECEC earns.

Head Start and licensed centers must meet staff qualifications established by state and local licensing in most states. Some states do not license part-day programs. Head Start must also meet the national Head Start Performance Standards and the new Congressional mandate requiring college degrees for 50% of all classroom staff by 2003.

Status of ECEC workers appears to correlate with college credit, so that policies that offer more training require more competence, and workers with this training may in the end command higher salaries. There are several innovative approaches to compensation. Some of these approaches may be enacted into statute, but most are implemented by administrative order or through licensing rules, which have the force of law. Labor unions have played only a small part in policy development for the ECEC work force because nationally, most ECEC is not unionized. The staying ability of the union, however, has made union leaders in ECEC remarkably effective. Massachusetts, for example, has had two wage initiatives led by its ECEC union.

Family child care providers are organized as private membership associations at the local level, loosely connected with a national organization. Family child care providers in general are considered self-employed. When they are part of an agency that recruits homes and places children, the agency may call them independent contractors. The Internal Revenue Service, however, may consider agency-related family child care providers to be employees of the agency, regardless of what the agency calls them. If the agency sets the providers' hours or fees, tells them how to do the work, how many children they can accept, and collects the money from parents, then the agency is likely to be found to be the employer.

In an earlier era, providers were often recruited by the state and considered to be state employees. Family child care was not widely used, except for with child welfare problems. A few states may still retain that earlier concept of the relationship. If family child care providers are state employees, they can be covered by state benefits, which is a decided advantage to these providers. For these providers to be state employees, the state would have to set their fees, define their work, set their hours, tell them how many and which children to enroll, and collect the money.

There is now a new reason for putting effort into working out these relationships so that family child care providers could be classified as state employees. That is the initiative in Rhode Island, spreading to other states, of covering family child care providers, and possibly center staff, with the state employees' benefit program.

Some other innovations to improve compensation to ECEC staff include the following:

- Provider Merit Pay Awards are available in Montana.

- The Wisconsin Quality Improvement Grants Program has funds for family child care homes and ECEC centers.

- The Rhode Island legislature is considering legislation to cover ECEC center staff with state insurance.

- The Wayne County Health Choice program in Michigan offers HMO-like health care coverage to low-wage employees of ECEC centers, restaurants, beauty salons, and other establishments that do not offer medical benefits. This policy was designed to help hospital costs by reducing the number of uninsured individuals who are treated but cannot pay their bills.

- The Child Care W.A.G.E.S. Project in Orange County, North Carolina, provides salary supplements to preschool teachers and family child care providers who earn less than $10.94 per hour and directors earning less than $11.68 per hour; these supplements are tied to the individuals' levels of education.

It is possible to use a "Big Picture" chart (see Table 5.1) to develop a fair and rational salary schedule in which salaries are equitable across the different systems.

THE MILITARY SYSTEM
AS MODEL FOR THE FUTURE

The Military Child Care Act of 1989 (PL 101-189) provided federal dollars for the different branches of the armed services to develop a system of ECEC options, with its own regulatory system, training, improved wages, and accreditation. This program has become a model for success and demonstrates improved workforce policy for the ECEC system. Civilian programs can now observe a large-scale program that is adequately funded, that addresses quality, that has reasonable personnel policies, and that serves all children. This is one of the largest employer-sponsored ECEC programs in the world, serving approximately 200,000 children every day.

Some of the features of this program are as follows:

- There is a common regulatory infrastructure for accountability, integrated service delivery in centers, family child care, school-age programs, and resource and referral.

- Each inspection has a "fix, waive, or close" policy.

- Approximately 75% of programs are accredited from outside the military, at national standards.

- The work force is professionalized, with competency-based training modules following the CDA functional areas and ongoing training 24 hours per year.

- Wages and wage advancement are tied to staff education and performance.

- There has been a dramatic reduction in turnover, following training and wage improvements.

- Service is available to all military children, with no "gap group" of families who are unable to pay but ineligible for subsidized care.

LOOKING AHEAD

The most important reforms in the staffing system in the United States will result from concerted systemic planning across the three major systems that deliver ECEC. Three trends give reason for hope that change across systems will come about in time. The trends are as follows.

1. *Career development planning groups* in almost every state have formed and have begun to bring about changes. These groups originally formed in the early 1990s in most states. Since then they have begun to influence cross-system policies to make professional development more coherent for the public schools, Head Start, and the purchase-of-service system. Some of these groups' reforms have included identifying core competencies, developing career lattices, establishing registries for practitioners, increasing articulation from one level to another in higher education, creating director credentials and infant/toddler credentials, increasing funding for training and for scholarship help for college, increasing DOL apprenticeships in ECEC, crafting compensation improvement strategies, and placing a greater emphasis on quality in ECEC.

2. *Quality improvement initiatives* are being funded with dramatic increases in public dollars. These initiatives by states, using state and federal dollars, increased dramatically throughout the 1990s, but especially in the years 1997, 1998, and 1999. In those years, the states were mid-stream in their welfare reform and committed to using public dollars to strengthen all ECEC so that mothers could work. At first these initiatives were unconnected, but a pattern has begun to emerge that will bring these new policies into some coherent relationship to one another. Many of these initiatives were stimulated by career development advocacy groups.

3. *Community partnerships* have been initiated among Head Start, the public schools, and purchase-of-service ECEC, and some of these partnerships are becoming increasingly effective. Significant funds and policy decisions have been placed behind the effort to collaborate across systems at the local level. All three systems of care have made a serious commitment to collaboration. Just the fact that people are meeting locally to plan, whereas in the past they did not even know one another, is already bringing about greater collaboration. There are now joint training programs, scholarship funds, and efforts to improve quality across systems.

REFERENCES

Boston Early Education Quality Improvement Project. (1997). *Boston EQUIP brochure: Data for the city of Boston.* Boston: Associated Day Care Services.

Bureau of Labor Statistics. (1996). *Current data on child care salaries and benefits in the United States from the Center for the Child Care Workforce.* Washington, DC: Center for the Child Care Workforce.

Cost, Quality and Child Outcomes (CQO) Study Team. (1995). *Cost, quality and child outcomes in child care centers.* Denver: University of Colorado, Center for Research in Economics and Social Policy, Department of Economics.

Elementary and Secondary Education Act of 1965, PL 89-10, 20 U.S.C. §§ 241 *et seq.*

Final Rule–Head Start Program Performance Standards, 45 C.F.R. § 1304 (1996, November 5).

Military Child Care Act of 1989, PL 101-189, 10 U.S.C. §§ 113 *et seq.*

Morgan, G., Azer, S., Costley, J., Genser, A., Goodman, I., Lombardi, J., & McGimsey, B. (1993). *Making a career of it: The state of the states report on career development in early care and education.* Boston: Wheelock College Center for Career Development in Early Care and Education.

Washington, V., & Andrews, J.D. (1998). *The children of 2010.* Washington, DC: National Association for the Education of Young Children.

Whitebook, M., Howes, C., & Phillips, D. (1998). *Worthy work, unlivable wages: The National Child Care Staffing Study 1988–1997.* Washington, DC: Center for the Child Care Workforce.

6

Program Content
and Implementation

Lilian G. Katz

To a large extent, preschool and kindergarten settings in the United States are under the supervision of the separate states and various governmental agencies within them. As a matter of tradition and policy, these agencies do not include in their supervision specification of program content and implementation, although some of them offer general guidelines and recommendations. Thus, there is no national curriculum for preschool or kindergarten programs in the United States.

Precise data concerning program content and implementation in the many thousands of preschool and kindergarten settings across the country can only be inferred from the large descriptive literature on early childhood education and care (ECEC) practices. Trends based on this literature are noted next.

MAIN PHILOSOPHIES OR GOALS GUIDING
PROGRAM CONTENT AND IMPLEMENTATION

At least three major influences on ECEC content and practice should be noted. The first is the strong and increasing pressure to adopt program practices that are thought to best prepare preschoolers and kindergartners for the academic demands of the next level of education. This trend is usually referred to as *school readiness*. A second, parallel trend in the field is the so-called *push down* of the curriculum and its associated methods from the primary school to preschool and kindergarten. Thus, children younger than 6 years of age are increasingly expected to master basic literacy and numeracy skills previously introduced to children at or after reaching 6 years of age. Alongside these two trends, a third has been the growing and deepening awareness and appreciation of the cultural diversity of the nation's children and families and the urgency of addressing the implications of this diversity in both program content and teaching methods.

The first two trends have exacerbated the long tradition of dissension concerning philosophies, goals, and methods that has marked the field of ECEC in the United States from its beginning. Indeed, Roopnarine and Johnson observed that in the United States, ECEC is a "profession teeming with controversy, impassioned with deeply held convictions, and inspired by rival value systems" (1993, p. iii). These persistent disagreements concerning curriculum and methods in ECEC programs are related to many factors. Among them are ideological positions, competing theories of development and learning, and conflicting pressures from various stakeholders concerning the desired outcomes and effects of the programs.

The controversies have been stated in various ways. Some positions are stated in terms of the aims and goals of the programs, such as academic learning versus personal-social development (see Stipek & Greene, 2001). Some contenders define the issues in terms of the respective roles of the teachers and the children, such as teacher-directed versus child-initiated interactions (Marcon, 1999). Others express the issues in terms of the content or nature of the activities offered, such as core knowledge versus play (Goffin, 1994; Hirsch & Holdren, 1996). Growing interest in a *constructivist* approach to programs and methods suggests that the traditional controversies can be summarized as shown in Table 6.1.

INFLUENCES ON PRACTICES

Trends in ECEC practice are influenced in many ways. Historically, charismatic leaders such as Maria Montessori have drawn attention

Table 6.1. Common terms used to describe contrasting emphases to curriculum and teaching methods in early childhood education and care (ECEC) in the United States

Constructivist	Instructivist
Child initiated	Teacher initiated or directed
Child centered	Teacher centered
Play based, progressive	Didactic or traditional
Emphasizing personal-social development	Focusing on basic academic skills
Developmentally appropriate	Developmentally inappropriate
Process oriented	Product oriented
Informal/emergent	Formal/structured
Children "construct" their own knowledge.	Children gain core knowledge.

to new ways of thinking about the nature of childhood and adults' roles in nurturing children. Political and ideological forces have also played a large role in determining pedagogical practices. In addition, advances in various aspects of the developmental sciences can influence the kinds of experiences provided to children in ECEC environments, such as with the introduction of Piaget's theories to the United States in the 1960s.

Developmentally Appropriate Practice

On the basis of information available and taking into account the large number of ECEC settings across the country, it seems reasonable to assume that in spite of the sizable variety of well-developed curriculum models available, the majority of program practices are eclectic. That is, rather than follow a particular curriculum model, their common practices include regular opportunity for spontaneous play; some introduction to basic academic skills; and some group experiences with physical activities, music, art, and literature.

In 1987, the National Association for the Education of Young Children (NAEYC), however, made a major effort to resolve persistent controversies and to prevent the pushing down of the primary curriculum into the early years, representing the consensus of its more than 100,000 members. NAEYC's position statement, titled *Developmentally Appropriate Practice in Early Childhood Programs* (Bredekamp, 1987), was revised in 1997 (Bredekamp & Copple, 1997) in response to various criticisms. This very influential and widely adopted position statement and accompanying document does not claim to be a curriculum per se; rather, it is intended to provide criteria upon which to judge the appropriateness of any of the numerous curriculum approaches employed in the United States today. As many as 15 major varieties of curriculum approaches to ECEC have been identified (Goffin, 1994; Roopnarine & Johnson, 1993).

Head Start and the Ill Effects of Poverty

One of the major influences on the field of ECEC since the mid-1960s has been the acknowledgement that poverty frequently jeopardizes important aspects of development in various ways. The Head Start program serves more than 905,000 three- and four-year-old children of low-income families across the United States (U.S. Department of Health and Human Services, Administration on Children and Families, 2002). Funded by the U.S. Department of Health and Human Services, its goals are set out in the form of "performance measures" that all programs are expected to satisfy ("Final Rule–Head Start Program Performance Standards," 1996). The two main goals on which the performance measures are based are the development of "social competence" and of "school readiness" (p. 2). The performance measures were modified in 1998 to require that children master 10 letters of the alphabet as a criterion of successful completion of the Head Start program (Head Start Amendments of 1998, PL 105-285). Legislation has also extended Head Start benefits in a program called Early Head Start, a community-based program for low-income families with infants and toddlers that is designed to support the children's early development and promote healthy family functioning.

Other Influences on Early Childhood Practice

As stated previously, the literature on ECEC curriculum models suggests that there are at least 15 recognizable curriculum models or approaches to ECEC (Goffin, 1994; Roopnarine & Johnson, 1993). The proliferation of competing curriculum approaches to ECEC was so extensive during the 1960s and early 1970s that the U.S. Office of Education (now known as the U.S. Department of Education) and the Head Start Bureau launched comparative studies of the approaches' effects in the Planned Variation Experiment and in Project Follow Through. In her discussion of these studies, Goffin listed the following preschool models:

Bank Street College of Education Approach
Behavior Analysis Model
EDC [Education Development Center] Open Education Program
Englemann-Becker Model
High/Scope Cognitively Oriented Model
Individualized Early Learning Program
Interdependent Learning Model
Responsive Educational Program
Responsive Environments Corporation Early Childhood Model
Tucson Early Education Model (1994, p. 25)

Goffin's list did not include the Montessori method, which is still being implemented in some 4,000 schools in the United States. The Waldorf approach is also being implemented in 127 schools in the United States. In addition to serving older children, both Montessori and Waldorf schools serve preschool- and kindergarten-age children. Other approaches in use today include the Reggio Emilia approach, the Creative Curriculum, the Core Knowledge Curriculum, the Project Approach, and variations of a constructivist approach.

Several theorists are thought to have influenced the content and teaching practices in the field since the mid-1970s. For example, the High/Scope Foundation has trained more than 26,000 teachers to use its curriculum model based largely on Piagetian theory (Epstein, Schweinhart, & McAdoo, 1996). References to the theories of Piaget and Vygotsky continue to be common in the literature on ECEC curriculum and teaching methods.

In addition, since the 1990s many ECEC practitioners have been influenced by Howard Gardner's theory of multiple intelligences (Armstrong, 1994). Another growing trend in the United States is widespread interest in the impressive practices observed and documented in the infant-toddler and preprimary schools of the northern Italian city of Reggio Emilia (Edwards, Gandini, & Forman, 1998). Thousands of American early childhood educators have viewed the "Hundred Languages of Children" exhibit of Reggio Emilia children's work and have visited the schools in Reggio Emilia. (See Chapter 10 for further discussion of the Reggio Emilia approach and its influence on ECEC in the United States.)

ACCOMMODATING CHILDREN WITH SPECIAL EDUCATIONAL NEEDS

The U.S. government's role in the education of young children with special educational needs began in the 1960s with support for the training of teachers of children with speech difficulties. Services for children with special needs were expanded with the Education for All Handicapped Children Act of 1975 (PL 94-142), which was most recently revised as the Individuals with Disabilities Education Act (IDEA) Amendments of 1997 (PL 105-17). According to this law, states receive some funds from the federal government to assist in the education of those with special needs from ages 3 through 21. Therefore, all states provide services to preschoolers with identified special needs. In addition, the law provides states with some federal funds for early intervention services for infants and toddlers (birth to age 3 years) with special needs or those thought to be at developmental risk.

Least Restrictive Environment

As a result of federal and state regulations regarding IDEA 1997, many programs include children with special needs in their ECEC programs for typical children. This stems from the mandate, which appears in IDEA 1997 and was introduced in an earlier version of the law, that children ages 3 through 21 who have special needs be placed in the "least restrictive environment," with every possible effort made to place children with special needs alongside typically developing children when appropriate.

Inclusion Arrangements

Odom et al. (1999) described 10 types of approaches to the inclusion of children with special needs in programs serving typically developing children. They classified the 10 types of approaches into organizational and individualized strategies. Organizational contexts include community-based ECEC programs, Head Start, and public school classes. In addition, some children are enrolled in two programs simultaneously: one in which the children are included with typically developing children for certain parts of the day and another program designed to meet special needs for the rest of the day. Individualized service models included mainly an itinerant specialist engaged in periodic direct service, collaborative and consultation services, team teaching, or another arrangement that maximizes the inclusion of special needs children in the least restrictive environment.

RESPECTING AND VALUING ALL KINDS OF DIVERSITY

The trend toward greater attention to cultural and linguistic diversity across the country is being addressed by a variety of organizations, educators, and scholars too numerous to list here. This trend is also strongly supported by relevant governmental agencies and is a strong component of the Head Start program (see, e.g., Derman-Sparks, 1992; Lynch & Hanson, 1998). For example, when selecting reading materials for children in Head Start, teachers are encouraged to be sure to include books whose illustrations clearly incorporate characters who belong to the racial and ethnic groups represented in the classes. In addition, many children in Head Start are from single-parent families; story and reading materials are expected to include events and characters involving such families. Many Head Start classes include children for whom English is a new language. Programs are expected to ensure that adults who can understand the children's first languages are readily available to help with the situations that arise in the classroom and with the parents of such diverse groups.

With particular attention to cultural and linguistic diversity among children with special needs, the Early Childhood Research Institute on Culturally and Linguistically Appropriate Services (CLAS) at the University of Illinois at Urbana-Champaign identifies, evaluates, and promotes effective and appropriate early intervention and preschool practices that are sensitive and respectful to children and families of diverse backgrounds. Serving the entire country, CLAS aims to develop a resource bank of validated, culturally and linguistically appropriate materials and documents concerning effective strategies for aiding children who are developing typically and who have special needs. Information gained by collecting, reviewing, and cataloging the materials is then disseminated to practitioners who are concerned with the needs of children and families of all cultures and languages across the country.

EASING TRANSITIONS THROUGH EARLY CHILDHOOD EDUCATION AND CARE PRACTICES

Many specialists in ECEC consider the transition from early childhood settings to those of the more formal elementary schools a potential source of difficulty for young children. It was thought that these difficulties could be minimized by making the program content and implementation practices more continuous than they had usually been. The Follow Through program, funded and managed until the mid-1970s by the U.S. Office of Education, was the first major attempt to minimize the discontinuities and transition difficulties between preschool and school experiences by supporting the elementary schools in adopting the curriculum practices employed in Head Start. However, because evidence accumulated that many of the developmental gains observed in Head Start children seemed to subside after a few years in elementary school, Head Start began a comprehensive approach to supporting young children's transitions to school. This approach includes connections between the home, school, and community, with an effort to strengthen the continuity of experiences of the children.

Kagan (1992) pointed out that there are at least two types of continuity: horizontal and vertical. The horizontal dimension addresses the issues in transition between the settings, such as home, school, and neighborhood, that a child experiences simultaneously. Vertical continuity refers to transitions in school experiences, services, and personnel with whom children interact that occur in succession or sequences over time.

The Regional Educational Laboratories' Early Childhood Collaboration Network (1995) developed one innovative approach to addressing transition problems and ensuring horizontal continuity during transitions. The network identified eight elements that must be addressed to improve transitions for young children. These are 1) families as partners, 2) shared leadership, 3) comprehensive and responsive services, 4) home culture and language, 5) communication, 6) knowledge and skills development, 7) appropriate care and education, and 8) evaluation of partnership effectiveness. The framework includes detailed guidelines for participants in the transition processes to evaluate their progress and share their perceptions of the effectiveness of the tools it offers.

Another approach to managing the problems of horizontal continuity is the model of the School of the 21st Century Network. These schools are designed to promote the whole range of support services to children and their families, including adult education and prenatal care for expectant parents, through close linkage with community resources (Zigler, Finn-Stevenson, & Marsland, 1995).

Many preschools and elementary schools in the United States have begun to increase the vertical continuity of children's educational experiences by introducing the practice of "looping" of teachers. Looping is the practice of teachers moving with their pupils to the next class in 2 or more consecutive years. Burke (1997) stated that schools have reported positive effects on both student achievement and parental involvement as a result of the extended family aspect of looping. Along similar lines, the practice of mixed-age grouping has been reintroduced in preschools and in the primary grades of elementary school in support of a wide variety of potential benefits including improved continuity of experience and subsequent easing of transitions (Katz, Evangelou, & Hartman, 1990; Kinsey, 2001; Veenman, 1995).

SUMMARY

In a country with more than 22 million children younger than 5 years of age, most of whom participate in some kind of educational or child care setting, it is difficult to capture the diversity of approaches to program content and implementation. ECEC specialists in the United States constantly propose and undertake experiments by which to improve the quality of ECEC provisions.

REFERENCES

Armstrong, T. (1994). *Multiple intelligences in the classroom*. Alexandria, VA: Association for Supervision and Curriculum Development.

Bredekamp, S. (Ed.). (1987). *Developmentally appropriate practice in early childhood programs serving children from birth through age 8*. Washington, DC: National Association for the Education of Young Children.

Bredekamp, S., & Copple, C. (Eds.). (1997). *Developmentally appropriate practice in early childhood programs* (Rev. ed.). Washington, DC: National Association for the Education of Young Children.

Burke, D.L. (1997, December). *Looping: Adding time, strengthening relationships* (ERIC Digest). Champaign, IL: ERIC Clearinghouse on Elementary and Early Childhood Education. (ERIC Document Reproduction Service No. ED414098)

Derman-Sparks, L. (1992). "It isn't fair!": Antibias curriculum for young children. In B. Neugebauer (Ed.), *Alike and different: Exploring our humanity with young children* (Rev. ed.). Washington, DC: National Association for the Education of Young Children.

Education for All Handicapped Children Act of 1975, PL 94-142, 20 U.S.C. §§ 1400 *et seq.*

Edwards, C., Gandini, L., & Forman, G. (Eds.). (1998). *The hundred languages of children: The Reggio Emilia approach. Advanced reflections*. Stamford, CT: Ablex.

Epstein, A.S., Schweinhart, L.J., & McAdoo, L. (1996). *Models of early childhood education*. Ypsilanti, MI: High/Scope Press.

Final Rule—Head Start Program Performance Standards, 45 C.F.R. § 1304. (1996, November 5).

Goffin, S. (1994). *Curriculum models and early childhood education: Appraising the relationship*. New York: Macmillan.

Head Start Amendments of 1998, PL 105-285, 42 U.S.C. §§ 9831 *et seq.*

Hirsch, E.D., Jr., & Holdren, J. (Eds.). (1996). *What your kindergartner needs to know: Preparing your child for a lifetime of learning*. New York: Dell.

Individuals with Disabilities Education Act (IDEA) Amendments of 1997, PL 105-17, 20 U.S.C. §§ 1400 *et seq.*

Kagan, S.L. (1992). The strategic important of linkages and the transition between early childhood programs and early elementary school. In *Sticking together: Strengthening linkages and the transition between early childhood education and early elementary school. Summary of a National Policy Forum*. Washington, DC: U.S. Department of Education.

Katz, L.G., Evangelou, D., & Hartman, J.A. (1990). *The case for mixed-age grouping in early education*. Washington, DC: National Association for the Education of Young Children.

Kinsey, S.J. (2001). *Multiage grouping and academic achievement*. (ERIC Digest). Champaign, IL: ERIC Clearinghouse on Elementary and Early Childhood Education. (ERIC Document Reproduction Service No. ED448935) Also available on-line at http://ericir.syr.edu/plweb-cgi/fastweb?getdoc+ericdb2+ericdb+1053789+0+wAAA+%28Multiage%26grouping%26and%26academic%26achievement%29

Lynch, E.W., & Hanson, M.J. (Eds.). (1998). *Developing cross-cultural competence: A guide for working with children and their families* (2nd ed.). Baltimore: Paul H. Brookes Publishing Co.

Marcon, R. (1999). Differential impact of preschool models on development and early learning of inner-city children: A three cohort study. *Developmental Psychology, 35*(2), 358–375.

Odom, S.L., Horn, E.M., Marquart, J.N., Hanson, M.J., Wolfberg, P., Beckman, P., Lieber, J., Li, S., Schwartz, I., Janko, S., & Sandall, S. (1999). On the forms of inclusion: Organizational context and individualized service models. *Journal of Early Intervention, 22*(3), 185–199.

Regional Educational Laboratories' Early Childhood Collaboration Network. (1995). *Continuity in early childhood: A framework for home, school, and community linkages*. Retrieved July 29, 2002, from http://www.sedl.org/prep/hsclinkages.pdf

Roopnarine, J.L., & Johnson, J.E. (Eds.). (1993). *Approaches to early childhood education*. New York: Merrill.

Stipek, D.J., & Greene, J.K. (2001.) Achievement motivation in early childhood: Cause for concern or celebration? In S.L. Golbeck (Ed.), *Psychological perspectives on early childhood education: Reframing dilemmas in research and practice* (pp. 64–91). Mahwah, NJ: Lawrence Erlbaum Associates.

U.S. Department of Health and Human Services, Administration on Children and Families. (2002). *2002 Head Start fact sheet*. Retrieved July 29, 2002, from http://www2.acf.dhhs.gov/programs/hsb/research/02_hsfs.htm

Veenman, S. (1995). Cognitive and noncognitive effects of multigrade and multi-age classes: A best-evidence synthesis. *Review of Educational Research, 65*(4), 319–381.

Zigler, E.F., Finn-Stevenson, M., & Marsland, K.W. (1995). Child day care in the schools: The school of the 21st century. *Child Welfare, 74*(6), 1301–1328.

7

Family
Engagement and Support

Barbara T. Bowman

This chapter gives an overview of how programs concerned with the development and education of young children have involved parents. Early childhood programs have had different purposes, have taken place under different auspices, and have changed over time; yet, over the past century two principles have guided national policies and practices and explain how and why programs in the United States have evolved the way they have.

PARENTS AND FAMILIES IN
EARLY CHILDHOOD PROGRAMS

Guiding Principles

The first and most important of these principles is the primacy of the parent–child relationship. Within broad limits, parents are considered the sole responsible agents for their young children. As children grow, other social institutions, such as schools, the police, and the courts, compete with parental authority to define children's care and education. Before children reach school age, however, parents traditionally have had full control over arrangements for children and can act in what they consider their children's best interests, without interference from others. This belief has changed somewhat over the past century, with a gradual recognition of the need for the other members of the community to assist parents in the effort to protect, care for, and educate young children. Nevertheless, the principle of parent responsibility has held steady, and the focus of early childhood programs has been to promote the bond between parents and their children. The primacy of parental responsibility has been matched by an equally prevalent belief that parents should be educated about how best to raise young children. In 1928 for example, William John Cooper, then U.S. Commissioner of Education, said, "No longer may we assume that it (parenting) is an inborn capacity. So to mother's heart must now be added mother's head" (Powell, 1991, p. 93). Throughout the 20th century, a barrage of information about child development and child rearing was directed at parents, and one of the most important sources of this information was programs devoted to early childhood education and care (ECEC).

Government Policy and Parental Authority

The belief in parental responsibility and authority drives any discussion of public versus private responsibility for providing and/or regulating ECEC. Historically, parents bore the full financial burden of their children's care and only when they were incapacitated did the church and charitable organizations provide assistance. During the 20th century, there was a gradual change in this belief as government assumed increasing responsibility for the health and education of children. Since the 1960s, government has added programs for low-income children; for children with disabilities; and, most recently, for working families to cover a larger share of these families' ECEC. Nevertheless, the public hesitancy about government involvement in ECEC continues. For example, public opinion rates parental choice as essential in early childhood programs, even though high costs and/or unavailable and inaccessible programs restrict many families' choices. (See Chapter 3 for further discussion of affordability of and access to ECEC.) Although there is a rising interest in and acceptance of public support to families for children through direct subsidies and tax benefits, the public still remains reluctant to provide support to mothers who work. In 1999, the majority of working parents thought that families should bear primary financial responsibility for their children's care while they are at work, whereas only 16% thought government should share the responsibility and favored tax credits for the care and education of children *if* the credits were available for working parents and parents who remain at home with their young children ("More Time Off for Kids," 1999). At present, government support to working parents, though increasing, is small in relation to the full cost of ECEC, and even former welfare recipients must bear an increasing share of their child care costs as they move into the minimum wage job market. Although these policies and opinions may reflect the American public's ambivalence about maternal employment, they certainly are consistent with the belief that families, not government, should be responsible for young children.

The belief in family responsibility is also reflected in the government's reluctance to regulate the quality of education and care children receive. There has been consistent unwillingness in most states to mandate high standards for ECEC through state licensing, despite the weight of evidence regarding the relationship of program quality to children's development (Howes, Phillips, & Whitebook, 1992; Peisner-Feinberg et al., 1999). This hesitation may be due, in part, to the desire of parents and service providers to contain cost, but it also responds to the public's wish not to usurp the right of parents to decide on the types of arrangements they wish to make for their children. Therefore, the primary legislated restrictions on family choice usually are only health and safety standards. (Chapter 4 contains further discussion about licensing and regulation of ECEC programs.)

FAMILY INVOLVEMENT IN PROGRAMS FOR YOUNG CHILDREN

Nursery Schools

Over the 20th century, three forms of out-of-home programs have provided care and education for young children. One type, often called *nursery school* or *preschool,* is designed to provide socialization and educational experience for 3- to 5-year-old children. Usually a half-day in length, 2–5 days a week, nursery programs have been organized under the auspices of churches and other not-for-profit groups, located primarily in middle-income communities, and paid for by parents. They have offered numerous opportunities for parents to be involved with their children, including in the role of teacher.

Government Programs

A second type of early childhood program is government sponsored. Until the 1960s, government programs were temporary and designed to meet national emergencies, such as during the economic depression of the 1930s and when women were needed to work during World War II. These programs were as concerned with adult needs for employment as with the developmental needs of children and reflected the belief that children's education and care were not paramount in their own right but could be included in a program to benefit the adult community.

Public support for government involvement in ECEC was revived in the 1960s and 1970s as research spelled out the benefits of addressing children's developmental and learning difficulties early in childhood. The major national initiatives were Head Start for children from low-income families, which began in 1966, and special education for children with disabilities, which started in 1975 and gradually extended to include preschool-age children. Head Start, a component of the federal government's War on Poverty, provides ECEC and associated services for low-income children and their families. Special education, created through the Education for All Handicapped Children Act of 1975 (PL 94-142), which was most recently amended and reauthorized as the Individuals with Disabilities Education Act (IDEA) Amendments of 1997 (PL 105-17), provides services to children with diagnosed disabilities and those who are at significant developmental risk and their families. The programs for both low-income children and children with disabilities are funded in part by federal, state, and local governments and are subject to federal and state case law regarding eligibility and inclusion in programs; to federal and state regulations regarding the program structure; and, in the case of programs serving children with disabilities, to local school board implementations of these mandates. There is considerable variability in programs from state to state and from one locality to another. Head Start and special education programs, however, both reflect the principles of parental authority and parent education. The programs are voluntary, and parents are left to decide whether their children should be enrolled. Parents also play a leading role in determining services, and both types of programs are mandated to provide parent education.

Child Care

The third type of program is child care, or full-day care. Throughout most of the 20th century, charitable organizations provided places to stay for children whose low-income families worked or were distressed and/or dysfunctional. Some of these programs provided parent education and support as a part of their services, but the primary focus was on the safe and humane care of the children—what is often termed *custodial care*—with minimum attention to the children's cognitive development or school-related education. As increasing numbers of women joined the work force in the 1980s, the shift from mother to "other" care mushroomed and many more children were enrolled in child care programs. Since the mid-1970s, increasing research demonstrated that the quality of these programs determined whether they were beneficial or hazardous to the development of young children. Nevertheless, the emphasis on custodial care has lingered, primarily because of the expense of high-quality care (see Chapter 1).

Parents bear most of the expense of child care. Since the mid-1990s, the government has increased its allocations through income tax exemptions and tax credits and direct payments to low-income parents as they cycle off of welfare but makes few stipulations as it does with other programs, such as in Head Start and special education. As a rule, parent involvement, education, and support have not been strong components of child care programs. Unlike nursery schools that see parent education as an important part of their mission, child care programs tend to make few demands and offer few opportunities to parents to be involved. Voluntary accreditation plans, however, such as the one managed by the National Association for the Education of Young Children (1998), include parent involvement as an important aspect of high-quality care.

EXTENT AND FOCUS OF PARENT INVOLVEMENT IN EARLY CHILDHOOD EDUCATION AND CARE

The extent of family involvement in ECEC is as diverse as the environments in which children are cared for and educated. Variations depend upon the program focus (e.g., custodial child care, early intervention, education), the socioeconomic status of program participants, and the legal or operational requirements of the service providers. Different programs may offer an array of services to families; others provide only one type of service. Occasionally, participation in a parent program is a condition for a child's enrollment in an ECEC program; however, for the vast majority, participation in a parent program is voluntary. At minimum, most programs offer parents conferences about the progress of their children and opportunities to discuss particular problems and get referrals if necessary. Parent education also is quite common in all types of centers, as are chances to volunteer in the classroom and go on field trips. Programs use a variety of social activities to engage families, such as sponsoring suppers; providing sitters so that parents, including unmarried fathers, can attend parent meetings; and organizing support groups for custodial grandparents.

ECEC programs with mandated parent involvement, such as Head Start and programs offering special education or early intervention services, provide education and technical assistance to encourage parents in their decision-making roles. These provide social, health, and psychological family services; require opportunities for parent involvement and decision making; and sponsor parent education.

Despite the diversity of family services offered by ECEC programs, one way of categorizing these services is by their purpose. These include 1) *education* for parents to improve their child rearing, 2) *empowerment and advocacy* for low-income families and families of children with special needs, and 3) *support* to stabilize or improve family functioning.

Parent Education

ECEC programs have used a variety of methods of providing education to parents.

1. *Education for parenting:* Beginning early in the 20th century, government pamphlets, popular magazines, and books and pronouncements by pediatricians persuaded mothers to prepare for their child-rearing roles by informing themselves about child development and scientifically based child rearing practices. In early childhood centers, parent education activities included observation and participation in the classroom under the guidance of a teacher; lectures on child development and family life; and exhortations by professionals in medicine, psychology, and child development about how to raise healthy children. During the 20th century, the content of parent education programs moved from attention to physical health (sanitation and inoculations) early in the century, to mental health (relationships and emotional well-being) at mid-century, to cognitive and social development (school success and social tractability) as the century ended. Although much has changed over the years, improving child rearing through the dissemination of child development information and child-rearing recommendations continues to be a major focus. Concern about American educational competitiveness has provoked interest in child literacy, numeracy, and competence in science, and these subjects are often part of the parent education program, particularly for parents of children at academic risk.

2. *Personal growth:* ECEC centers also may use a range of opportunities for personal development to engage parents and bring them into the center. These may include instruction in handicrafts, personal grooming, cooking, and making clothing and self-help programs.

3. *Home visiting:* Home visiting is another way of reaching and educating parents. One such program, Parents as Teachers First, which is sponsored by the Chicago public schools, seeks to promote positive parenting and promote school readiness. The program trains community parents to visit the parents of infants and toddlers and teach the new parents how to interact with their young children so that the children will be ready for school. Another example is Parents as Teachers, provided by the Missouri Department of Elementary and Secondary Education. This program has four components:

- A home visit by a credentialed parent educator, who provides information, suggests activities, and responds to parents' questions and concerns

- Group meetings in which parents share observations and provide mutual support

- A monitoring system in which parents and home visitors both check children's progress

- Referrals, when necessary, to other community services

A number of different models of home visiting programs are now being evaluated. In general, home visits by professionals have been more successful in achieving their goals than have programs using less well-trained visitors (Behrman, 1999). A few programs have demonstrated modest but meaningful effects on children. The most successful ones are those with interventions of substantial length and intensity and with well-educated and trained visitors (Baker, Piotrkowski, & Brooks-Gunn, 1998).

4. *Adult education:* The strong tie between the formal education of caregivers (parents and teacher/providers) and child achievement (Bowman, Donovan, & Burns, 2001) has led programs for low-income parents to promote adult education. High school equivalence classes, child care programs in high schools for teenage parents, and child care in community colleges are designed to increase parents' formal education. Low-income parents who are also ECEC workers may receive compensation for taking college courses in child development and early education.

5. *Outreach:* Mothers are usually the primary participants in parent education programs, but recently programs have tried to reach new audiences. Fathers have become a focus of attention, particularly in programs serving teenage mothers. Other programs have extended their services to extended families. Drug addiction, incarceration, and abuse and neglect judgments have increased sharply since the early 1990s, and as a consequence, many children are in the care of grandparents and other family members. Also, some agencies provide parent education and support services in prisons and drug rehabilitation

facilities to maintain the parental relationship and to prepare parents to reassume family responsibilities.

Family Empowerment and Advocacy

Family empowerment as a focus for parent programs in ECEC environments evolved during the 1960s with the establishment of Head Start. Research showed that children whose parents were actively involved in institutions providing for their children's education and care were more successful in school (Mistry, Crosby, Huston, Casey, & Ripke, 2000; Seefeldt, Denton, Galper, & Younoszai, 1999). Parent empowerment and advocacy was also an important component of the community action focus of Head Start, which encouraged low-income families to mobilize to solve problems affecting their children. It was assumed that families and communities exercising political and social will would gain an enhanced sense of efficacy, improve community services, and become better role models for children. The encouragement of parents as empowered activists on behalf of their children remains a powerful objective for many programs for low-income families.

Similarly, an essential aspect of the special education legislation is the prominent role for parents as advocates for their children. Parents are required to "sign off" on educational decisions affecting their children, and if parents believe that the decisions do not meet their children's needs, the parents have the legal right to challenge these decisions. Thus, parent empowerment and advocacy are as important in the IDEA 1997 system as they are in Head Start.

Family Support

A more recent approach to parent involvement evolved in the 1980s and stressed the family rather than the child as the recipient of services. This approach views children as a part of a family system that is primarily responsible for their health and well-being; therefore, families need to be strengthened so that children can prosper. Parents not only need information about child development and optimal child rearing and need opportunities for empowered advocacy but also must find rewarding work, a supportive social life, and respect for family choice and decision making—components of a healthy self-image (Salisbury & Dunst, 1997; Weissbourd, 1990). Activities in family support centers are diverse and may include providing parents with information, social support, consultation, and relief from child rearing and encouraging decision making in all aspects of their lives. All parents, rich and poor and without regard to ethnicity, are seen as needing support; only the type of support varies for different parents.

A family support program may be a part of an early childhood center that offers a program to children, or it may be independent and offer a drop-in playroom for children while the parents participate in the program. Family support activities may include informal socialization, lectures, crafts, used clothing and toy sales, field trips, and social and psychological referrals for parents and children. Although many support programs cater primarily to mothers during the day, others include evening activities for working fathers and mothers. Increasingly, family support programs offer services to fathers, grandparents, and caregivers who care for young children in the children's homes.

Variation in Family Involvement

In real life, these different types of parent involvement (parent education, family empowerment and advocacy, and family support) often occur together. For example, one purpose of a special education or early intervention program is to ensure that children's parents know and exercise their responsibility as their child's advocate. But, a family with a child who has a disability may require a range of support and education services to cope with the stress of the child's disability. Similarly, many nursery schools maintain contact with mental health specialists, who can assist parents who are having personal difficulties and whose children need to be evaluated for disabilities or developmental delays.

Despite increases in the number of preschool children in center-based care, the majority of young children are cared for in unregulated homes, with 61% of children receiving care in their own or someone else's home (Capizzano, Schmidt, & Sonenstein, 1999), where the involvement of parents is not easily assessed. Family child care programs do not usually have formal parent programs unless the programs are attached to a network, in which case parents may participate in programs run by the central agency. Home-based care is informal, particularly when members of the child's family provide the care. It might seem likely that this form of care would offer maximum opportunity for parental input, but the dynamics of interpersonal relationships and the lack of parental choice regarding the type of ECEC used may limit parental influence.

BARRIERS TO PARENT INVOLVEMENT

There are many barriers to successful parent involvement in their children's ECEC. Among these are diversity of parental expectations, poor program conceptualization and implementation, parental reluctance to participate, and insufficient public support.

Diverse Expectations

Parents' expectations for ECEC are enormously diverse. Some parents expect no more than that their children are safe, whereas others want an educational program in an emotionally and socially supportive environment. Preference for particular arrangements or types of programs may vary depending on a family's ethnic, cultural, and socioeconomic background. Some prefer center-based to home-based ECEC or vice versa; some prefer part-day educational programs, whereas others want full-day care. Some parents expect teachers to "know" how to care for and educate the children and do not expect to participate unless there is a problem. Other parents want to be involved in decisions about all areas of their child's care and education while their son or daughter is in the care of others. Many parents use teachers and caregivers as sources of information and reassurance; others feel teachers do not understand their perspectives or problems. The diversity of parental expectations makes involving parents difficult.

Poorly Conceptualized and Executed Programs

Although research on child development shows a high correlation between family characteristics and children's development, engaging parents in a way to promote these positive outcomes has not proven to be easy (Behrman, 1999; St. Pierre, Layzer, Goodson, & Bernstein, 1997). Some programs falter because staff are inadequately trained as noted by the home visiting research (Baker et al., 1998). Providers also may apply policies and practices that work well in one community but not in another that differs by culture, language, or socioeconomic status, thus making a poor match between program resources and participant needs. Given that evaluations show that most models of parent involvement are ineffective in obtaining the desired outcomes, the quality of conceptualization and implementation of services would seem to be important factors. (See Chapter 6 for further discussion of program implementation.)

Reluctance of Parents to Participate

Another barrier to parent involvement in ECEC can be the parents' belief system and lifestyle, which may preclude involvement. Time constraints, cultural and linguistic differences, mental and physical health problems, and lifestyle conflicts are common. For instance, the parents of a child with a disability have the right to take part in educational decisions, yet they may feel uncomfortable in the institutional world of the school/center and refuse to participate. Less often considered are world views about the nature of problems and the purpose of intervention. For example, some parents believe in the immutability of children's cognitive skills and see little point in the type of readiness activities outlined by teachers. Others have different expectations for their children's development and may not be interested in promoting their child's independence, for instance. In other cases, parents not wish to participate because they do not value parent involvement activities and do not see how the activities are relevant to their lives. Adapting involvement activities to the cultural and personal realities of families is often unsuccessful.

Insufficient Public Support

Although family involvement in their children's education and care often is considered a high priority, public policies are inconsistent across levels of government and types of programs. For example, federal legislation for Head Start and IDEA 1997 mandate the right of parents to participate in program decisions, whereas other federally funded programs, such as the Child Care and Development Fund, have no such requirement. States also have weak and inconsistent mandates. Illinois, for instance, requires that state-funded preschools for children at risk of developmental delays provide parent involvement opportunities yet has no parent involvement policy for state-funded child care programs.

Few employer practices actively encourage and facilitate parents' involvement in the care and education of their young children and, in some instances, may discourage it. Employers, for instance, may pressure workers into overtime work and diminish the time available for parents to participate in center programs or may refuse parents time off with pay to attend program functions.

STRATEGIES TO
INCREASE PARENT INVOLVEMENT

There are both formal and informal systems to inform parents about ECEC options. In some localities, governmental officials have mounted campaigns to encourage employers to free working parents to attend their child's school two or three times a year for teacher reports and conferences, and many companies follow this practice. Some companies and governmental units have on-site ECEC programs and encourage parents to visit their children at lunchtime or during other free time during the day. (See Chapter 5 for information on the ECEC services offered to families in the military.)

Child Care Resource and Referral Agencies

Each state has a child care resource and referral (CCR&R) service, funded in part by federal funds, with agencies located in different areas of each state. All parents can get information from CCR&R agencies about cost, quality, and availability of different forms of ECEC. (See the section in Chapter 4 called "Mechanisms for Providing Consumer Information" for further discussion of dissemination of information to parents through CCR&R agencies.) Low-income families who are eligible for tax-supported subsidies also can obtain information and, in some states, vouchers to pay for their children's care. In addition, parents can use many informal avenues to find information, including advertisements in newspapers, posters on bulletin boards in grocery stores and Laundromats; flyers from community centers and public schools; and person-to-person communication among families, friends, and neighbors. It is interesting that most studies show that no matter how parents find their child education and care provider, they express satisfaction with their choice.

Employer Support

The ability of families to be involved in the education and care of their young children is directly related to their socioeconomic status. Families that are stretched financially often do not have the time or energy to be personally involved with their children, much less participate in programs. The most far-reaching public policy promoting parenting by reconciling work and family responsibilities is the Family and Medical Leave Act of 1993 (PL 103-3), which requires employers of more than 50 to grant workers up to 12 weeks' unpaid leave during any 12-month period. Leave time may be used to recover from illness or to care for ill family members and for newborn and newly adopted children. Employers are required to maintain employee eligibility for health benefits during the leave and return the worker to similar work and pay.

Private employers' support for parents is extremely variable. Some employers offer as much as 6 months' maternity leave with full pay and allow flexible work schedules for multiple years, whereas others are reluctant to reinstate employees who have taken unpaid leave. Family friendly policies include permitting employees to use sick days to care for a sick child, offering special ECEC arrangements for employees who must travel or work late, allowing flexible work schedules, and providing paid paternity leave for fathers. Employer decisions regarding support for parents are often based on the value of the worker (particularly women) to the company, the scarcity of workers in a particular field, and the likelihood of legal action. Despite improvements, many American families are experiencing considerable stress as they attempt to balance work and family.

Government Policies

New government tax policies, such as income tax credits or exemptions, withdrawals from tax-free accounts, and flexible spending accounts, provide some economic help to parents. Another governmental requirement, establishing paternity at birth, has increased the collection of awarded child support payments from noncustodial fathers, providing more options for custodial mothers. Although few in number, in general, government policies have moved in the direction of providing parents with both more time and more money to devote to ECEC.

Volunteering

The most widespread method by which ECEC programs engage community members, including the families of the children served, is through volunteer programs. Volunteerism has a long history in the United States, and many early childhood service providers, including Head Start, hospitals, settlement houses, and places of worship, regularly recruit community volunteers to assist with ECEC programs.

Collaboration

Another widely used approach is community collaboration in which human service organizations work together to streamline delivery and avoid duplicating resources. For instance, schools in some communities, such as schools in Kentucky, have become full-service centers for the coordination of delivery of heath, welfare, and social services, promoting one-stop support for families. Community collaborations are often encouraged by federal, state, and local governments, which either require or encourage cooperative efforts.

Another model of community collaboration seeks to transfer some of the responsibility for social programs from government to community-based organizations. These organizations are encouraged to define problems and find solutions, receive and distribute funding, and evaluate programs (University of Chicago, Chapin Hall Center for Children, 1997). Such initiatives are designed to build human capital by strengthening all sectors of the social, educational, economic, physical, and cultural environment. It has been difficult to judge the effectiveness of these community-based initiatives on children's well-being, but evaluation efforts have offered opportunities to explicate theories of change and to understand and evaluate complex and diverse family support programs (Kagan, 1998).

SUMMARY

Child and family problems are not new. As in the past, some families are overwhelmed with the stress of balancing the daily demands of work and child rearing with too few human and material resources and need child care. Low-income families, who often deal with a host of other conditions, such as increased interpersonal friction, violence, and untreated physical and mental health conditions, need health and social services to ameliorate the effects of poverty on their children. School achievement is no longer an option, and ECEC programs can be instrumental in getting children ready for school. And, parents continue to need education, support, and opportunities for empowered advocacy as children grow and develop in healthy environments.

What is new is the increasing recognition that helping parents needs to be a community responsibility. Early childhood programs can supply much of the help needed by families. ECEC programs form a diverse system, providing multiple and flexible supports for both children and families. ECEC programs, however, must look back over their traditions and achievements and ahead to new challenges and new strategies to help families. Early childhood programs can be a great investment for the future if we develop new public policies, new early childhood practices, and new outreach to families based on the traditional principles of supporting child–family relationships and providing parents with education and support.

REFERENCES

Baker, A.J.L., Piotrkowski, C.S., & Brooks-Gunn, J. (1998). The effects of the Home Instruction Program for Preschool Youngsters (HIPPY) on children's school performance at the end of the program and one year later. *Early Childhood Research Quarterly, 13,* 571–588.

Behrman, R. (Ed.). (1999). Home visiting: Recent program evaluations. *The Future of Children, 9*(1).

Bowman, B.T., Donovan, M.S., & Burns, M.S. (Eds.). (2001). *Eager to learn: Educating our preschoolers.* Washington, DC: National Academy Press.

Capizzano, J., Schmidt, S., & Sonenstein, F. (1999). *Preschoolers in non-parental child care: A preview of NSAF's child care data.* Washington, DC: Urban Institute Press.

Education for All Handicapped Children Act of 1975, PL 94-142, 20 U.S.C. §§ 1400 *et seq.*

Family and Medical Leave Act (FMLA) of 1993, PL 103-3, 5 U.S.C. §§ 6381 *et seq.,* 29 U.S.C. §§ 2601 *et seq.*

Howes, C., Phillips, D., & Whitebook, M. (1992). Thresholds of quality: Implications for the social development of children in center-based child care. *Child Development, 63,* 449–460.

Individuals with Disabilities Education Act (IDEA) Amendments of 1997, PL 105-17, 20 U.S.C. §§ 1400 *et seq.*

Kagan, S.L. (1998). Using a theory of change approach in a national evaluation of family support programs: Practitioner reflections. In K. Fulbright-Anderson, A.C. Kubisch, & J.P. Connell (Eds.), *New approaches to evaluating community initiatives: Vol. 2. Theory, measurement, and assessment.* Aspen, CO: The Aspen Institute.

Mistry, R., Crosby, D., Huston, A., Casey, D., & Ripke, M. (2000). Lessons from New Hope: The impact on children's well-being. *Poverty Research News, 4*(4), 6–7.

"More time off for kids." (1999, July 7). *Report on Preschool Programs, 31,* 111.

National Association for the Education of Young Children (NAEYC). (1998). *Guide to accreditation by the National Association for the Education of Young Children: 1998 edition.* Washington, DC: Author.

Peisner-Feinberg, E., Burchinal, M., Clifford, R., Yazejian, N., Culkin, M., Zelaszo, J., Howes, C., Byler, P., Kagan, S., & Rustici, J. (1999). *The children of the Cost, Quality and Child Outcomes Study go to school: Executive summary.* Chapel Hill: University of North Carolina at Chapel Hill, Frank Porter Graham Child Development Institute.

Powell, D.R. (1991, July). *Strengthening parental contributions to school readiness* (Paper commissioned by the Office of Educational Research and Improvement). Washington, DC: U.S. Department of Education.

Salisbury, C.L., & Dunst, C.J. (1997). Home, school, and community partnerships: Building inclusive teams. In B. Rainforth & J. York-Barr, *Collaborative teams for students with severe disabilities: Integrating therapy and educational services* (pp. 57–87). Baltimore: Paul H. Brookes Publishing Co.

Seefeldt, C., Denton, L., Galper, A., & Younoszai, T. (1999). The relation between Head Start parents' participation in a transition demonstration, education, efficacy and their children's academic ability. *Early Childhood Research Quarterly, 14,* 99–109.

St. Pierre, R., Layzer, J., Goodson, B., & Bernstein, L. (1997). *The effectiveness of comprehensive care management interventions: Findings for the national evaluation of the comprehensive child development program.* Cambridge, MA: Abt Associates.

University of Chicago, Chapin Hall Center for Children. (1997). *The partnership for neighborhood initiatives: Report of the Chapin Hall Center for Children at the University of Chicago.* Chicago: University of Chicago, Chapin Hall Center for Children.

Weissbourd, B. (1990). Family resource and support programs: Challenges in human service. The schools and family-oriented prevention. In D. Unger & D. Powell (Eds.), *Families as nurturing systems* (pp. 157–174). New York: Haworth Press.

8

Funding Issues for Early Childhood Education and Care Programs

W. Steven Barnett and Leonard N. Masse

Early childhood education and care (ECEC) policies in the United States are fragmented, inconsistent, and inadequately funded (Barnett, 1993). The same can be said of statistical information about ECEC, which makes producing definitive and up-to-date descriptions of funding and policy very difficult. One important step toward coherent policy would be the development of a better statistical base to assist in decision making about ECEC policies and programs in this field. Since the 1990s, some steps have been taken in that direction. A prominent example is the National Household Education Survey (NHES), a national survey of household behavior. Conducted by the National Center for Education Statistics, the first NHES took place in 1991 and focused on adult education and early childhood program participation. The NHES has also been conducted in 1993, 1995, 1996, 1999, and 2001 and has focused on adult education, civic involvement, library use, school readiness, school safety and discipline, before- and after-school programs, and early childhood program participation. Specifically, household-reported data on ECEC program participation were collected in 1991, 1995, 1999, and 2001. Parents or households, however, are not a reliable

---

Unless otherwise noted, all dollar amounts in this chapter are reported as 2002 dollars.

source of information on the structure, operation, and financing of ECEC programs, and even data on program use are not collected annually. This chapter seeks to present the best data available, but the limitations of this data make the case for an improved ECEC statistics system.

BACKGROUND

ECEC is an area of public policy in which education and child rearing intersect. A lack of understanding about the importance of formal education for young children (even early childhood educators tend to be hostile toward the phrase *formal education*) has led policy making to be dominated by views about child rearing. Political ideology in the United States emphasizes the primary responsibility of the family for child rearing to an even greater extent than it does for education (see Chapter 7). The roles of government are limited to 1) assisting all families in meeting their responsibilities by reducing their tax burden (tax exemptions and tax credits for children that are not tied to use of child care), 2) assisting families who cannot fulfill their responsibilities due to the extraordinary circumstances of poverty or a child's disability, and 3) regulating providers (typically only commercial providers) of ECEC services (see Chapter 4 for further discussion of regulation of ECEC). Regulation is primarily a state government responsibility. There is a strong tendency in regulated industries for the regulatory agencies to more strongly represent the interests of the providers (owners and operators, who are politically active and well organized) rather than the consumers. ECEC is similar to other regulated industries in these respects. The result is often less emphasis on consumer issues related to program quality and more emphasis on producer issues related to program finance and operations.

Despite the rhetoric of ECEC and the genuine overlap in the services provided, differences between the two domains of education and care create problems for analysis. Child care policy and programs are administered by one set of agencies, education by another, and Head Start (a "child development" program) by another. These agencies have different reporting requirements, different constituencies, different views of what are the most important program goals and of what constitutes a quality program, and even different views about the appropriate role of the government. This presents problems for producing a consistent set of information about these programs. Moreover, it highlights the issue of the substantial heterogeneity among programs. Studies clearly show that Head Start programs provide substantially higher quality education on average than do child care and other preschool programs that operate as licensed child care centers (Barnett, Tarr, & Frede, 1999; Zill et al., 1998). The primary reasons for this are the higher level of funding and more stringent program standards imposed by Head Start. Similar data are not available on programs that operate under the auspices of the public schools, but the higher level of funding and higher standards suggest that they also may be of higher quality (though not uniformly so).

Child care is not an early childhood service per se; rather, it is a service for children as old as 14, and data often are not available only on preschool-age children. Even when data are available, there are limitations to their usefulness. For example, Head Start and preschool education programs serve children who have not yet entered school. There is no clear age limit here, however, as some children enter kindergarten at age 4 and other children remain in preschool programs at age 5. The minimum age for entrance into kindergarten is age 5 in most states. The cutoff date used to determine entrance age differs from state to state, and can even vary across school districts in the same state (Education Commission of the States, 2002). The actual age at which a child may enter kindergarten is also influenced by the age at which a child is legally required to attend school. As stated in Chapter 1, compulsory school attendance age ranges from 5 to 8 years of age. Despite these differences across the states, however, 96% of kindergarten children who began school in the fall of 1998 were younger than 6 years upon entrance (Zill & West, 2001). These interstate differences, however, are large enough to create some uncertainty as to the exact definition of the preschool population and to a corresponding set of age cohorts that can be employed in state and national analyses.

SOURCES OF FUNDING

Household, federal government, and state government spending in 1995 on ECEC for children from birth through age 4 in the United States amounted to about $40 billion. As can be seen in Table 8.1, this reflects a considerable increase from 1992, the other year for which complete estimates could be obtained. It should be noted that these figures differ from estimates that combine spending on child care for children of all ages with spending on the education of children younger than 5 years. This chapter focuses on resources devoted to the care and education of children younger than 5 years. The amount spent on *preschool* children is somewhat higher than our estimate because that would include perhaps one quarter of 5-year-olds and a small number of 6-year-olds. Spending is not always reported by age, and a substantial amount of care is in the underground economy. The precision of our estimates is limited by these and other problems with the available data.

We found a large increase in private spending from 1992 to 1995, although some of the difference may be due to differences in the method of estimation. In fiscal year 2001, government provided perhaps $25 billion, with $16 billion from the federal government and as much as $9 billion from state and local governments. If past trends

Table 8.1. Major sources of expenditures on early childhood education care (ECEC; amounts are in billions of 2002 dollars)

Source	1992		1995	
	Amount	%	Amount	%
Households	17	57	24	60
Federal government	9	30	11	28
State government	4	13	5	12
Total	30	100	40	100

Sources: Household expenditures for 1992 are estimated based on expenditures presented in Stoney and Greenberg (1996) for 1991. Household expenditures for 1995 are based on data from the 1995 National Household Education Survey (NHES; National Center for Education Statistics, 1997). Household expenditures have been reduced by the amount of federal tax credits for each year. Federal government expenditures are from Center for Early Education Research (CEER; 1999). State government expenditures represent spending on federal matching programs, state prekindergarten initiatives, and state spending for children with disabilities from birth through age 4. State expenditures on federal matching programs for 1992 are from Hayes and Danegger (1995), and the expenditures for 1995 are estimated from data presented in Stoney and Greenberg (1996) and the U.S. Department of Health and Human Services ([HHS], 1998).

had continued, parents would have paid as much as $30 billion in 2001, after subtracting the tax credits from their payment amounts. This would yield a total expenditure of $55 billion for 2001. According to our estimates, families pay just around 55%, the federal government pays about 30%, and state and local governments pay about 15% of the costs of ECEC. As shown later in this chapter, funding is not evenly distributed but is focused on particular populations (children from lower income families and children with disabilities). Contributions from philanthropy could account for perhaps 1%–5% of spending but are difficult to estimate from reports from ECEC centers.

Our estimates understate the true costs of ECEC for several reasons. First, our estimates do not include the value of lost income or leisure time to parents, relatives, and others who take time out of the labor force and other activities to care for and educate young children. Second, the estimates do not include costs to teachers who (out of charitable interests) work in ECEC at wages below what they could earn in other occupations. Finally, they do not include the value of cash and in-kind donations to programs that come primarily from local charities and individuals.

PRIVATE FUNDING

Using data from the 1995 NHES (National Center for Education Statistics, 1997), we estimate that households in the United States paid about $24 billion for the care and education of children younger than 5 years of age in 1995, after adjusting for tax credits. This compares with an estimate of $17 billion for 1992 that is obtained from Stoney and Greenberg (1996) after adjusting their figure for child care tax credits received by households in 1992. It might be argued that child care tax credits should not be deducted from parent expenditures because households view the credits as an increase in their income and not government payments that decrease their child care expenditures. Tax credits, however, would then not properly be considered government contributions to funding child care. Failure to deduct tax credits, therefore, from household expenditures results in a double counting of these amounts and an overestimation of household expenditures on child care.

Care provided in an ECEC center is one particular child care arrangement for which there is some information on funding sources. There is less information on other arrangements, including care by relatives, friends, sitters, and family child care homes. Data from a survey of a nationally representative sample of ECEC centers indicate that centers serving young children receive about 70% of their revenue from private fees, about 15% from the government, and about 15% from other sources (Morris, Helburn, & Culkin, 1995). In ECEC centers that serve low-income families, parent fees are sometimes set on a sliding scale. Federal law requires that programs funded under the Child Care and Development Fund (CCDF; discussed later) take income and the number of children in the household into account in setting parent fees.

FEDERAL GOVERNMENT FUNDING

Although there are dozens of federal programs involved in funding ECEC, 10 account for the vast majority of the funds. Table 8.2 presents estimates of the funds that each of these programs spent in 2001 and in earlier years on children birth to age 5. As many of these programs are not limited to children younger than 5, Table 8.3 presents total funding for each program across all age groups (birth to age 14) with an indication of the age group to which the funding applies.

Federal funding for the care and education of children younger than 5 has grown steadily since the mid-1970s. The programs that have contributed to this growth, however, have varied over time. In the 1980s, funding increased largely as a consequence of growth in the amount spent on the Child and Dependent Care Tax Credit (CDCTC). Use of the CDCTC fell dramatically after 1988, when taxpayers were first required to report the social security number of the ECEC provider. The number of taxpayers applying for the credit in 1989 dropped by one third from the prior year. How much of the drop was due to a reduction in false reports of child care and how

Table 8.2. Federal expenditures on early childhood education and care (ECEC) for children younger than 5 years of age, selected programs and years (millions of 2002 dollars)

Program	1973	1977	1988	1992	1995	1999	2001
Head Start	1,409	1,277	1,584	2,702	3,973	4,992	6,224
Child Care and Development Fund (CCDF)				1,196	1,632	2,357	3,056
Social Services Block Grant (SSBG)	933	1,536	643	550	317	204	178
Child and Dependent Care Tax Credit (CDCTC)	611	926	3,331	2,186	2,120	1,753	1,579
Dependent Care Assistance Plan (DCAP)					511	286	335
Even Start				86	116	148	251
Individuals with Disabilities Education Act (IDEA) of 1990 and Amendments of 1997—Part B				216	224	220	229
IDEA—Part C				214	358	396	427
Child and Adult Care Food Program (CACFP)		229	570	973	1,187	1,127	1,140
Title I	133	—	—	658	678	713	704
Temporary Assistance for Needy Families (TANF)						1,380	2,267
Total	3,086	3,968	6,128	8,781	11,116	13,576	16,390

Sources: With the exception of data for IDEA expenditures, data for 1973–1992 are from Barnett (1993) and Children's Defense Fund (1992). IDEA data for 1992 were obtained directly from the Office of Special Education Programs, within the U.S. Department of Education (USDOE; 1992). With the exception of data for Title I, data for 1995 are based on those presented in Stoney and Greenberg (1996). Expenditures for Title I for 1995 are based on data available from the USDOE (2001b). Expenditures for 1999 for Head Start, CCDF, SSBG, CDCTC, Even Start, and IDEA Parts B and C are from the Office of Management and Budget (OMB; 1999). DCAP expenditures for 1999 and 2001 are from the Joint Committee on Taxation (1998, 2001). Expenditures for 1999 for Title I are from the *FY 1999 Budget Summary* (USDOE, 1999). Expenditures for 1999 and 2001 for CACFP were obtained from the Food and Nutrition Service of the U.S. Department of Agriculture (2002). Head Start expenditures for 2001 are from the Head Start Bureau of the U.S. Department of Health and Human Services (HHS; 2002a). CCDF, CDCTC, and SSBG expenditures for 2001 are from the OMB (2001). Title I, Even Start, IDEA Part B, and IDEA Part C expenditures for 2001 are from the OMB (2002). TANF expenditures for 1999 are from Gish (2002) and for 2001 are from Schumacher (2002).

Table 8.3. Federal expenditures on child care and early education for children younger than 14 years of age, selected programs and years (millions of 2002 dollars)

Program	Ages served	1973	1977	1988	1992	1995	1999	2001
Head Start	Birth to 5	1,409	1,277	1,584	2,702	3,973	4,992	6,224
Child Care and Development Fund (CCDF)	Birth to 14				1,793	2,448	3,535	4,584
Social Services Block Grant (SSBG)	Birth to 14	1,400	2,304	964	825	476	306	267
Child and Dependent Care Tax Credit (CDCTC)	Birth to 14	916	1,388	4,997	3,279	3,180	2,630	2,369
Dependent Care Assistance Plan (DCAP)	Birth to 14					766	429	502
Even Start	3–5				86	116	148	251
Individuals with Disabilities Education Act (IDEA) of 1990 and Amendments of 1997—Part B	3–5				393	408	401	416
IDEA—Part C	Birth to 3				214	358	396	427
Child and Adult Care Food Program (CACFP)	Birth to 14		343	855	1,459	1,781	1,691	1,710
Title I	3–4	133	—	—	658	678	713	704
Temporary Assistance for Needy Families (TANF)							2,070	3,400
Total		3,858	5,312	8,400	11,409	14,184	17,311	20,854

Sources: With the exception of data for IDEA expenditures, data for 1973–1992 are from Barnett (1993) and Children's Defense Fund (1992). IDEA data for 1992 were obtained directly from the Office of Special Education Programs, within the U.S. Department of Education (USDOE; 1992). With the exception of data for Title I, data for 1995 are based on those presented in Stoney and Greenberg (1996). Expenditures for Title I for 1995 are based on data available from the USDOE (2001b). Expenditures for 1999 for Head Start, CCDF, SSBG, CDCTC, Even Start, and IDEA Parts B and C are from the U.S. Office of Management and Budget (OMB; 1999). DCAP expenditures for 1999 and 2001 are from the Joint Committee on Taxation (1998, 2001). Expenditures for 1999 for Title I are from the *FY 1999 Budget Summary* (USDOE, 1999). Expenditures for 1999 and 2001 for CACFP were obtained from the Food and Nutrition Service of the U.S. Department of Agriculture (2002). Head Start expenditures for 2001 are from the Head Start Bureau of the U.S. Department of Health and Human Services (HHS; 2002). CCDF, CDCTC, and SSBG expenditures for 2001 are from the OMB (2001). Title I, Even Start, IDEA Part B, and IDEA Part C expenditures for 2001 are from the OMB (2002). TANF expenditures for 1999 are from Gish (2002) and for 2001 are from Schumacher (2002).

much to tax avoidance by ECEC providers cannot be determined. In later years, Head Start and welfare reform were responsible for much of the growth in federal funding.

Except for the tax credit and the Dependent Care Assistance Plan (DCAP; discussed later), federal spending is heavily targeted on lower-income families. Despite this it seems likely that families with lower incomes still pay a relatively high percentage of their income for ECEC. In the early 1990s, families *paying for the care and education* (some families paid nothing) of preschool children and earning less than $1,200 per month (in 1995 dollars) paid 25% of their incomes for ECEC (Casper, 1995). In comparison, families paying for care and earning more than $4,500 per month (in 1995 dollars) paid only 6% of their incomes for ECEC (Casper, 1995). The structure of current programs, however, leads to inequities with respect to ECEC service delivery and pricing among families with similar levels of income. For example, Head Start and child care programs lack sufficient funding to serve many eligible families.

Head Start

Investment in early care and education began on a large scale with the Head Start program in 1965. Head Start is a federally funded program that is targeted at low-income families. ECEC is primarily provided for a half-day to children 3–4 years of age. The program's goal is to improve the general experiences and environment of children who are at risk of developmental delay and/or school failure. Grants are awarded to local organizations that are interested in establishing Head Start programs. There is no fee to households of participating children, but the program is generally subject to a 20% local match. The match can take various forms, including direct funds from the local source or in-kind labor and physical resources, including the labor of volunteers from the community and participating households; or the matching requirement may be waived entirely. Compared with the quality of child care programs, the quality of educational services provided by Head Start is relatively high. Head Start is also successful in seeing that children receive health, dental, and other services.

- Federal funds for Head Start in 2001 were $6.2 billion (U.S. Department of Health and Human Services [HHS], 2002a).

- Head Start funds are targeted at ECEC (birth to age 5); therefore, the values in Tables 8.2 and 8.3 are equal in value.

- Head Start was expanded in 1994 to include Early Head Start, for children younger than 3 years and their families. In 2000, funding for Early Head Start programs equaled $423 million, approximately 8% of the total Head Start budget (HHS, 2001).

- Funding increases have been used to raise quality and to increase the numbers of children served.

Child Care and Development Fund and Temporary Assistance for Needy Families

Coincident with welfare reform in 1996, Congress reauthorized and revised the Child Care and Development Block Grant (CCDBG), the primary ECEC subsidy program operated by the federal government. The expanded CCDBG is also referred to as the Child Care and Development Fund (CCDF). The CCDF provides federal funds to states for child care subsidies for families with incomes less than or equal to 85% of the state's median income. Subsidy recipients must either be working or "preparing to work." States are provided mandatory, matching, and discretionary funds. States must devote no less than 70% of mandatory and matching funds to ECEC assistance to families who are receiving public assistance (Temporary Assistance for Needy Families [TANF]; described next), families who are attempting to go off public assistance, or families who are at risk of becoming dependent on public assistance.

The 1996 welfare reform law (Personal Responsibility and Work Reconciliation Act of 1996, PL 104-193) formally replaced the Aid to Families with Dependent Children (AFDC) program (authorized under Title IV-A of the Social Security Act) with a new block grant to states, called TANF (still under Title IV-A). TANF combines assistance to families with more stringent work requirements. TANF funds can be used in many areas, including prevention of pregnancy, job assistance, family formation and maintenance, and child care

(HHS, 2002b). Beginning in the late 1990s, TANF provided substantial funds for child care through direct expenditures to welfare recipients and through state transfers of TANF funds to CCDF (Gish, 2002). TANF transfer funds to CCDF can be used to fund child care for families who do not qualify for assistance under the TANF program.

- Federal CCDF funds for 2001 were $4.6 billion (Office of Management and Budget [OMB], 2001).[1]

- States may contribute and request matching funds.

- Federal TANF funds for child care for 2001 were $3.4 billion (Schumacher, 2002).

- It is estimated that two thirds of funds for child care are spent on children younger than 5 years old (Barnett, 1993). With this figure, the ECEC estimates for CCDF and TANF in 2001 were $3.1 billion and $2.2 billion, respectively.

Social Services Block Grant

The Social Services Block Grant (SSBG) was authorized under Title XX of the Social Security Act. The law provides grants to states for providing social services that are determined to be appropriate by states. Various sources have estimated that 15% of funds are spent on child care and early education (GAO, 1998; House Committee on Ways and Means, 1998).

- Federal funds for SSBG in 2001 were $1.8 billion (Office of Management and Budget [OMB], 2001).

- Federal funding for child care (birth to age 14) and early education was $267 million (15% of total).

---

[1]To make estimates meaningful over time, the value for CCDF prior to 1996 in Tables 8.2 and 8.3 is the sum of the funds allocated to CCDBG, the AFDC Jobs Program, the Transitional Child Care Program, and the At-Risk Child Care Program.

- Federal funding for ECEC (birth to age 5) was $178 million (two thirds of the amount given in Table 8.3).

- No state matching funds are required.

Child and Dependent Care Tax Credit

The CDCTC provides a reduction in tax liability (tax credit) for child care expenses. The credit may be claimed by married couples when both spouses are either working or attending school full-time. It may also be claimed by divorced, separated, or single parents with child custody.

- Estimated credit for child care (birth to age 14) and early education in 2001 was $2.4 billion (OMB, 2001).

- Estimated credit for ECEC (birth to age 5) in 2001 was $1.6 billion (two thirds of the amount given in Table 8.3).

- Some states have similar credits, but these generate far less funding.

Dependent Care Assistance Plan

The Dependent Care Assistance Plan (DCAP) allows taxpayers to exclude from taxable income contributions for child care expenses. Unlike a tax credit, which reduces the amount of an individual's tax but not his or her taxable income, the federal DCAP program mirrors similar state programs and permits individuals to deduct child care expenses up to $5,000 directly from taxable income. If a taxpayer applies for a DCAP reduction in taxable income, then there are limitations on the amount of the CDCTC that can be claimed. Specifically, child care expenses that are included in a DCAP cannot also be claimed as expenses for tax credit purposes. DCAP figures reported by the Joint Committee on Taxation are adjusted to reflect the reduction in the use of the CDCTC.

- Federal funding for child care (birth through age 14) and early education in 2001 was $502 million (Joint Committee on Taxation, 2001).

- Federal funding for ECEC (birth to age 4) in 2001 was $335 million (two thirds of the amount given in Table 8.3).

Even Start

Even Start is a family literacy program for low-income families and their children. Even Start was authorized in 1989 under the auspices of the Elementary and Secondary Education Act of 1965 (PL 89-10). Even Start is federally funded with local grants to projects administered by the states. The projects have three basic components, focusing on adult education and literacy, parenting education, and early childhood education. Even Start programs serve children from birth to age 7, although the majority of children are younger than 6 years of age (St. Pierre, Gamse, Alamprese, & Rimdzius, 1998). The three components target directly or indirectly the development of the young children, either through early education and care or through the education and training of parents.

* Expenditures for 2001 were $251 million (OMB, 2002).

* Estimate is the same for both Table 8.2 and Table 8.3.

IDEA Part B — Preschool Grants

Part B of the Individuals with Disabilities Education Act (IDEA) Amendments of 1997 (PL 105-17) provides for a Preschool Grants program for children between 3 and 5 years of age who require special education and related services. Programs are administered by the states through local early care and education programs. Eligible children are placed in the least restrictive environment that is appropriate for the delivery of the services needed by the children; approximately 75% of preschool children served under IDEA Part B in 1998 were placed in an early childhood classroom setting (U.S. Department of Education [USDOE], 2001a).

* Estimate for 2001 funding of child care (birth to age 14) and early education was $416 million (OMB, 2002).

* Estimate for ECEC (birth to age 5) is 55% of the total given in Table 8.3 based on the percentage of children under the age of 5 served by the program. Data on program participation is available

in the reports to Congress on the implementation of IDEA (USDOE, 1992, 1995, 1997, 2001a).

- Estimate for 2001 funding of ECEC was $229 million.

IDEA Part C—Grants for Infants and Toddlers

Part C of IDEA 1997 provides for grants for infants and toddlers (birth to age 3 years) with disabilities and those deemed to be at risk of developmental delays. Similar to programs funded through Part B grants, Part C early intervention programs are administered by the states, and eligible children receive services in "natural environments," which may include the home and settings in the community. Because younger children are more likely to be cared for in the home setting, the law requires that this setting be an option for parents of children receiving services funded by IDEA Part C. In 1998, approximately 78% of eligible children received services in a home-based setting (USDOE, 2001a).

- Estimate for 2001 ECEC funding was $427 million (OMB, 2002).
- Estimates for Table 8.2 and Table 8.3 are equal in value because IDEA Part C serves only children younger than 3 years of age.

Child and Adult Care Food Program

The Food and Nutrition Service of the U.S. Department of Agriculture administers the Child and Adult Care Food Program (CACFP). This program provides food and reimbursements for food served to low-income children in ECEC (and to a few adults in daytime care).

- Estimate for 2001 funding of child care (birth to age 14) and early education was $1.7 billion (U.S. Department of Agriculture, 2002).
- The *1998 Green Book* of the House Committee on Ways and Means estimated that 98% of CACFP funds were allocated to children and 2% were allocated to adults. In addition, two thirds of the amount given in Table 8.3 was assumed to be for children under the age of 5.
- The 2001 estimate for ECEC (birth to age 5) was $1.1 billion.

Title I

Title I of the Elementary and Secondary Education Act of 1965 (PL 89-10), Education for the Disadvantaged, provides funding to schools based on the percentage of economically disadvantaged students served. Title I estimates for ECEC for 1995 and 1999 are based on an average of 8% of total Title I resources. An unweighted average of 2% was used in a report issued by the GAO and was based on the ratio of children receiving child care services to the total number of children served by Title I (GAO, 1998). We estimated a weighted average based on an average cost of child care services equal to $5,000 and calculated that the percentage of resources devoted to child care was equal to 14%. The former method assumes that child care expenditures are uniform across all age groups. The latter method assumes that all children between the ages of 3 and 4 receive full-day preschool. Because neither assumption is perfectly accurate, we chose to employ the arithmetic mean of the two estimates. The ECEC estimate is used in Table 8.3 as well and likely underestimates Title I funding for child care and early education.

- The 2001 estimated appropriation was $8.8 billion (OMB, 2002).

- Assuming 8% of the total is for ECEC, then the 2001 estimate is $704 million.

STATE AND LOCAL GOVERNMENT FUNDING

State and local government (school districts and municipalities) spending on ECEC is less than federal spending. We estimate that it approached $9 billion in 2001. Our estimate is larger than most previous estimates, but funding has been increasing and past estimates did not include preschool special education. The relative roles of the various levels of government in funding ECEC differ from the situation in education finance for public education generally. In elementary and secondary education, the federal role in education funding is quite small, and state and local governments bear most of the burden. Because a large amount of state and local spending on

ECEC programs is not centrally reported, it is difficult to estimate the state and, especially, the local share of funding. Thus, we have produced estimates for state and local funding that include most state spending plus local school spending on special education for children birth to age 4. This omits some local school and municipal funding for ECEC. The omitted funding, however, is not likely to be a substantial percentage of the total.

The primary areas of state (and local) funding are child care, preschool education programs, and preschool special education programs. State funding for child care is primarily associated with the federal CCDF and TANF programs, which seek to leverage state spending by requiring a state match and evidence of maintenance of state effort. State child care spending tends to be for low-income families in the form of vouchers or direct payments to child care providers. State child care funding was estimated to have risen to about $2.7 billion by 2000 (Gish, 2002). In addition, 39 states and the District of Columbia support preschool education programs of some sort, either as independent programs or as a supplement to Head Start (Olson, 2002). These programs mostly target low-income children or children otherwise designated as at high risk of school failure. Funding for these programs has increased dramatically since the late 1980s. State funding for preschool education programs was approximately $277 million in 1988, and this has grown to close to $2 billion in 2002, with the funding levels varying considerably from state to state (Mitchell et al., 1997; Mitchell, Ripple, & Chanana, 1998; Sandham, 2002; Schulman, Blank, & Ewen, 1999). In addition to offering regular preschool education programs, all states provide preschool special education programs for young children with disabilities and developmental delays. We estimated state (and local) funding for preschool special education to be about $4.3 billion in 1999 (see Tables 8.4a and 8.4b). This estimate was calculated by estimating the total cost of serving children enrolled in these programs and subtracting the federal funding provided for these programs. Finally, state tax credits and deductions for child care add perhaps $250 million, if one extrapolates from the early 1990s and subtracts amounts applying to older children (Stoney & Greenberg, 1996).

The rise in state funding of early childhood education in the 1990s coincided with a movement toward universal preschool pro-

Table 8.4a. State and local funding of pre-school programs for children ages 3–4 with disabilities (data are in millions of 2002 dollars)

Year	Amount
1992	$2,030
1995	$2,514
1999	$2,941

Sources: Data are based on the number of 3- and 4-year-olds that have been served (U.S. Department of Education [USDOE], 1997) under the Individuals with Disabilities Education Act (IDEA) and Amendments of 1997 Part B Preschool Grants program. The number of children for 1999 is linearly estimated based on prior years. The state share of preschool expenditures is estimated by subtracting the federal share from an estimate of the total cost of preschool. The total cost is estimated by multiplying the number of 3- and 4-year-olds served under Part B by an average for the per-child cost of preschool. The federal expenditures for preschool come from the IDEA annual reports (USDOE, 1992, 1995, 1997).

Table 8.4b. State and local funding of pre-school programs for children ages birth to 2 with disabilities (data are in millions of 2002 dollars)

Year	Amount
1992	$955
1995	$1,074
1999	$1,373

Sources: Data are based on the number of children that have been served (U.S. Department of Education [USDOE], 1997) under the Individuals with Disabilities Education Act (IDEA) and Amendments of 1997 Part C Infants and Toddlers program. The number of children for 1999 is linearly estimated based on prior years. The state share of preschool expenditures is estimated by subtracting the federal share from an estimate of the total cost of preschool. The total cost is estimated by multiplying the number of children from birth to 2 years old served under Part C by an average for the per-child cost of preschool. The federal expenditures for preschool come from the IDEA annual reports (USDOE, 1992, 1995, 1997).

grams in a number of states. The programs are targeted mainly at 4-year-olds. The states with relatively large preschool programs include Georgia (one of several states moving toward universal preschool education), California, Florida, Michigan, Massachusetts, New Jersey, North Carolina, Ohio, and Texas. Some states are moving toward blending funding for child care and preschool education, as is the case in New Jersey's court-ordered "Abbott" district preschool programs. (In 1998, the New Jersey Supreme Court ordered the state to provide access to a high-quality preschool education for all 3- and 4-year-olds in 30 low-income school districts [Abbott districts].)

RESPONSIVENESS OF LABOR FORCE PARTICIPATION AND THE DEMAND FOR CHILD CARE TO CHILD CARE SUBSIDIES

Although a number of researchers have taken up the issue over the years, it is difficult to produce convincing estimates of the effects of subsidies for ECEC on parental employment. To date, there is no experimental evidence to bring to bear. Thus, we must rely on econometric estimates of how much any given policy change influences employment, and these estimates are highly sensitive to assumptions about measures, the specification equations, and the sources of the data (Kimmel, 1998). Moreover, researchers differ in how they portray their results, with similar estimates viewed as implying substantial responsiveness to price or policy changes by some researchers and small or negligible responsiveness by others.

There is general agreement that employment is responsive to the cost of ECEC and that employment of low-income women is more responsive than the average. Estimated elasticities of maternal employment with respect to price of ECEC range from 0.2 to 0.7, meaning that a 10% decrease in the cost of ECEC would produce a 2%–7% increase in employment (GAO, 1994). Blau and Hagy (1998) estimated that full subsidization of ECEC would lead to a 10% increase in labor force participation for all women. Kimmel (1998) found that the effects of ECEC prices are different for single and married mothers. She estimated that a 10% decrease in price would increase labor force participation by 2% for single mothers and 9% for married mothers. Cackley (1994) estimated that making ECEC free would increase labor force participation of all low-income mothers from 29% to 44%. This is a large change for these women, a 50% increase in the number of women in this group participating in the labor force.

There is general agreement that the effects of changes in the price of ECEC on the type of ECEC used are larger than the effects on employment (Hofferth, 1999). For example, Blau and Hagy (1998) estimated that full subsidization of ECEC would lead to a 20% increase in the use of paid care. Subsidies also seem likely to produce changes in the types of ECEC used, with families moving toward center-based and family home care and away from other forms (Hofferth, 1999).

In our view, one should not put too much trust in these econometric estimates. For policy purposes, one must extrapolate far beyond existing circumstances with respect to the availability of high-quality programs and the level of subsidy. One must also take into account that learning and attitude changes are likely to occur. For example, the take-up rate for Georgia's program for 4-year-olds has risen steadily. In New Jersey, one urban public school offering a full-day, extended-year program beginning at age 4 has far more applicants than it has available spaces. Apparently, the perception is that close substitutes are not available elsewhere. Enrollment rates are nearly 100% (universal) for preschool programs in some European countries (Tietze & Cryer, 1999). We think that this provides evidence of the potential for a large response to increased quality offerings. This can be particularly true if programs meet the educational needs of children and the specific needs of working parents and are based in a setting that the parents trust. As such programs are now rarely available, it is unlikely that this response could be estimated from existing data sets. Of course, increased child participation in ECEC does not guarantee parent participation in the labor force.

In addition, existing estimates tell us primarily about participation rates. Total hours may be more relevant, especially in the form of movement toward extended part-time and full-time work that can lift families out of poverty. The available estimates, however, indicate small responses in terms of hours worked for those already employed. Other aspects of employment that might be affected are absenteeism, employment continuity, and immediate and long-term productivity (Hofferth, 1999). Whether changes in all of these would be large enough to warrant a particular policy decision depends on the private and public benefits from increased earnings and productivity. Moreover, policy changes in the United States, such as paid parental leave, could increase both maternal employment and maternal investment in children, partly through increased time with children and partly through increased childbearing by older, more educated women (Gustaffson & Stafford, 1998). To our knowledge, no one has estimated these benefits so that, with benefits for child development, they could be compared with the costs of subsidizing high-quality ECEC for either lower-income women or the general population.

COSTS OF SUBSIDIZING
HIGH-QUALITY PROGRAMS

There is a lack of general agreement about the level of quality that it is desirable for ECEC in the United States (see Chapter 2 for a discussion of defining quality). Yet, quality must be specified to estimate cost. Many existing statements about quality represent political calculations about what is currently acceptable and concerns about the impact of raising standards on existing providers of services and are shaped by evidence regarding the effects of programs on child development and well-being. One contender for a consensus about quality is provided by the National Association for the Education of Young Children (NAEYC; 1998) accreditation standards. Our view is that NAEYC accreditation standards set a floor below which quality should not be allowed to fall rather than a goal to which programs should aspire.

Information on the implications of accepting NAEYC accreditation as a standard can be obtained from a GAO (1990) survey of NAEYC-accredited, full-day, year-round centers serving 4-year-olds (and children of other ages) in 1988. The average cost of these programs was $4,200 per child in 1988 dollars, including only purchased resources. About $600 in additional resources was donated, bringing the total estimated cost to $4,800. It is noteworthy that there is substantial regional variation in cost from $5,610 in the northeast to $4,500 in the west. Converted to 2002 dollars, the average cost would be about $6,750 per year.

As might be expected from the cost figures, the accredited programs did not fare well with respect to characteristics that are known to be associated with the quality of services provided to children. Teacher salaries in these programs were about half of public elementary school teacher salaries, and half of the teachers had a 4-year college degree of any type. National studies have found that 40%–50% of teachers in child care programs have 4-year college degrees (Kisker, Hofferth, Phillips, & Farquhar, 1991; Saluja, Early, & Clifford, 2002). Accredited programs may be somewhat better than others, but do they measure up to what we want for our children? Certainly, teacher qualifications in many of these programs would not be acceptable qualifications for being a kindergarten teacher. Why should they be acceptable for being a teacher of younger children?

Barnett (1998) and Frede (1998) have shown that there is a large gap between the quality of programs that research has shown to provide substantial gains for young children in poverty and the quality of typical Head Start and public school programs. This gap seems likely to be responsible for these programs' lower effectiveness. The quality of the typical child care center attended by children in low-income families is much lower even than the typical Head Start program (Barnett et al., 1999). Of course, the quality of child care generally is quite low. Although it may not harm most young children, the current level of quality is not necessarily desirable because it does not optimally use the opportunity for education and because children may have better lives in higher quality programs even if this does not contribute to measurably better long-term development. Unfortunately, given the current research base, many questions remain for making an objective determination of the quality of programs "needed" by young children in general (much of the research has been conducted with children in poverty).

In order to provide a basis for estimating the costs of alternative public subsidies for ECEC, we have estimated the costs using three different estimates of program cost: $12,000 per child; $8,000 per child; and $6,000 per child. The $12,000 figure is in the ballpark of the costs of programs that research has shown to have large benefits for children in poverty and is the figure that we consider a reasonable goal for public policy. The $6,000 figure is about the cost of NAEYC-accredited centers and is a lower-bound estimate of the cost of providing a mix of part- and full-day programs. These figures must be taken as averages. In New Jersey, a relatively high-cost state, $6,000 per child would not be sufficient to provide a quality program. It would not even cover the cost of kindergarten or Head Start. In other states with lower costs, $6,000 per child might be enough to provide quality programs. Obviously, the $8,000 figure provides something in between in terms of quality, hours of service, and comprehensiveness of services.

Estimates of the costs of public subsidies using the three cost estimates and three alternative assumptions about the subsidy level are presented in Table 8.5. The three alternatives are a full subsidy, a full subsidy for families below the median income with a sliding scale above the median that cuts the subsidy in half by the 75th percentile, and a sliding fee scale across the entire income range that cuts the fee to half at the median income. These estimates assume 50% participation rates for children younger than 1 year, 75% for children ages 1 and 2, and 100% participation rates for children ages 3–5. It is assumed that about one quarter of 5-year-olds are preschool children. These assumptions can be varied to produce alternate estimates. These estimates are based on the population in 2000 (U.S. Bureau of the Census, 2002).

The public costs of universal subsidies range from about $200 billion annually to about $100 billion annually at full subsidy, down to approximately $50 billion annually for the lowest subsidy. At the very least, this implies more than doubling the existing level of public spending on ECEC. At most, it implies increasing it by an order of magnitude. It also suggests that the level of underinvestment in ECEC in the United States could be quite large. Clearly, the public costs fall if the subsidies are limited to particular age ranges or subpopulations. Thus, if full subsidies are limited to the lowest income quintile (poverty rates for young children have recently been about 20% or lower), and there are no partial subsidies, the full-subsidy figures can be divided by 5 to estimate the cost. If only children ages 3–5 are subsidized, then the cost ranges from about $105 billion to less than $55 billion for a full subsidy. Limiting subsidies to low-income children 3–5 would require a full subsidy slightly more than $20 billion for a high-quality intensive program and about $11 billion for a program of minimal quality. It follows that even tripling the Head Start budget would fall short of achieving the goal of providing all low-income children ages 3–5 with high-quality intensive programs. In addition, aside from Head Start, programs for low-income families are not always limited to families in poverty and also serve children outside this age range. Clearly, even highly targeted programs would require substantial increases to accomplish their stated goals for all eligible children. Taking this into account, current federal and state spending on programs for 3- to 5-year-old children from low-income families probably amounts to significantly less than the $11 billion figure.

Table 8.5. Estimates of universal preschool program subsidies' annual costs (2002 dollars)

Program One: Full-day, intensive program of high quality, estimated per-child cost of $12,000

Age of child (years)	Number of children (thousands)	Participation rate (%)	Total cost (billions of dollars)		
			S1	S2	S3
<1	3,806	50	23	17	11
1	3,820	75	34	26	17
2	3,790	75	34	26	17
3	3,833	100	46	34	23
4	3,927	100	47	35	24
5	991	100	12	9	6
Total			**196**	**147**	**98**

Program Two: Part- or full-day program of average to high quality, estimated per-child cost of $8,000

Age of child (years)	Number of children (thousands)	Participation rate (%)	Total cost (billions of dollars)		
			S1	S2	S3
<1	3,806	50	15	11	7
1	3,820	75	23	17	11
2	3,790	75	23	17	11
3	3,833	100	31	23	15
4	3,927	100	31	23	16
5	991	100	8	6	4
Total			**131**	**97**	**64**

Program Three: Program of average quality, estimated per-child cost of $6,000

Age of child (years)	Number of children (thousands)	Participation rate (%)	Total cost (billions of dollars)		
			S1	S2	S3
<1	3,806	50	12	9	6
1	3,820	75	17	13	9
2	3,790	75	17	13	9
3	3,833	100	23	17	12
4	3,927	100	24	18	12
5	991	100	6	5	3
Total			**99**	**75**	**51**

Source: Population estimates for number of children are from U.S. Bureau of the Census (2002).

Key: S1, full subsidy across all household income levels; S2, full subsidy for families with household income below the median level and 50% subsidy for families with household income at or above the median level; S3, 50% subsidy across all household income levels.

ALTERNATIVE APPROACHES
TO FUNDING AND FINANCING

The choice of funding and financing mechanisms is largely a political issue, not a technical one. To our knowledge there is no magic bullet, no untapped revenue source or means of funding that would make large public subsidies for ECEC significantly more attractive. The political will to provide such subsidies must be generated based on the expected benefits. Financing and funding mechanisms have relatively little impact on program benefits, though they can impact the distribution of benefits. Most ECEC programs are financed through general revenues. There are distribution issues with respect to the incidence of various taxes, but they are not straightforward. One cannot simply assume that income taxes are progressive and sales taxes regressive, for example. One state, Georgia, has designated the lottery as the source of revenue for its universal program for 4-year-olds. It is unclear, however, whether there is a lesson here for other states. The politics of finance at the state level are likely to be highly idiosyncratic.

A number of major alternative approaches have been suggested for improving the ECEC system in the United States (e.g., Barnett & Boocock, 1998; Bergmann, 1999; Gomby et al., 1996). One is paid parental leave. This could be funded directly by the government, through tax-sheltered savings, or through employer mandates, although such mandates are likely to produce undesirable employer and employee side effects (Barnett & Musgrave, 1991). Parental leave is particularly attractive for infants given the high cost of their care and the belief that professional caregivers do not provide much added value (Barnett, 1993).

Another alternative is a voucher program that simply transfers money to parents and allows them to choose programs (Barnett, 1993; Bergmann, 1999). Parents could be given vouchers through a social welfare or educational system much as they are now for subsidized child care or educational choice programs. A voucher-type system also could be set up that would allow parents to save funds in a tax-free account. Government contributions to the account could be made using a sliding scale in which government payments decrease with income and/or the government provides funds to match family contributions. Also, provisions could be made to link the voucher or matching funds to use of higher quality programs. This could help to protect the public interest in increasing the quality of education and care that young children receive.

Finally, there is the existing programmatic model that involves a mix of vouchers, direct payments to programs, and direct provision of services (e.g., through the public schools). Looking at the existing programs, it is striking that small federal contributions to preschool special education for children with disabilities have elicited relatively large state and local government expenditures. This suggests that the federal government might establish an entitlement to early childhood services for other children that takes force when states agree to accept federal funds for the program. One difficulty is that Head Start has always bypassed the states for political reasons. It may be difficult to accommodate its constituency in a program that does go through state government.

There are a number of state early childhood initiatives that might help inform public policy more generally through closer study. The program for 4-year-olds in Georgia is the most obvious because it is closest to achieving universality for an age group. New Jersey's urban preschool program also deserves study. The program was developed as a result of a New Jersey Supreme Court order to implement high-quality, intensive programs for one quarter of the state's 3- and 4-year-olds. Its goal is to level the playing field at school entry between urban poor and suburban wealthy. It is particularly interesting that New Jersey seeks to implement this program by bringing together child care, Head Start, and public school funding and programs in its most disadvantaged cities. Similar developments are taking place in Connecticut and New York, though on a smaller scale (as evidenced by funding levels). In all three of these northeastern states, there are already "exemplary" local efforts that can be examined to see how such an approach works. California is of interest because it has a history of supporting ECEC programs going back to the Great Depression and World War II and a commitment to achieving universal provision. Ohio is noteworthy for trying to expand programs based on Head Start. North Carolina provides an interesting example: A series of well-informed policy initiatives have focused on improving quality and expanding access that recognizes the importance of professional development and compensation. Finally, in Massachusetts, the state department of education has been aggressively pursuing an agenda of raising quality and increasing collaboration by providing additional resources to communities contingent on the development of cooperative agreements linking the public schools, Head Start, and community child care programs.

REFERENCES

Barnett, W.S. (1993). New wine in old bottles: Increasing the coherence of early childhood care and education policy. *Early Childhood Research Quarterly, 8,* 519–558.

Barnett, W.S. (1998). Long-term effects on cognitive development and school success. In W.S. Barnett & S.S. Boocock (Eds.), *Early care and education for children in poverty: Promises, programs, and long-term results* (pp. 11–44). Albany, NY: SUNY Press.

Barnett, W.S., & Boocock, S.S. (Eds.). (1998). *Early care and education for children in poverty: Promises, programs, and long-term results.* Albany, NY: SUNY Press.

Barnett, W.S., & Musgrave, G.L. (1991). *The economic impact of mandated family leave on small businesses and their employees.* Washington, DC: National Federation of Independent Business Foundation.

Barnett, W.S., Tarr, J., & Frede, E. (1999). *Early childhood education in the Abbott Districts: Children's need and the need for high-quality programs.* New Brunswick, NJ: Center for Early Education Research.

Bergmann, B. (1999). Making child care "affordable" in the United States. *Annals of the American Academy of Political and Social Science, 563,* 208–219.

Blau, D., & Hagy, A. (1998). The demand for quality in child care. *Journal of Political Economy, 106*(1), 104–146.

Cackley, A. (1994). *Child care subsidies increase likelihood that low-income mothers will work.* Washington, DC: U.S. General Accounting Office.

Casper, L.M. (1995). "What does it cost to mind our preschoolers?" *Current Population Reports,* No. P70-52. Washington, DC: U.S. Bureau of the Census.

Center for Early Education Research (CEER). (1999). *Federal expenditures on early care and education* (CEER Fact Sheet No. 1). New Brunswick, NJ: Author.

Children's Defense Fund. (1992). *The state of America's children–1992.* Washington, DC: Children's Defense Fund.

Education Commission of the States. (2002.) *Kindergarten: State characteristics.* Retrieved August 13, 2002, from http://www.ecs.org/clearinghouse/13/30/1330/htm

Elementary and Secondary Education Act (ESEA) of 1965, PL 89-10, 20 U.S.C. §§ 241 *et seq.*

Frede, E.C. (1998). Preschool program quality in programs for children in poverty. In W.S. Barnett & S.S. Boocock (Eds.), *Early care and education for children in poverty: Promises, programs, and long-term results* (pp. 77–98). Albany, NY: SUNY Press.

Gish, M. (2002). *Child care: Funding and spending under federal block grants* (CRS Report 31274). Washington, DC: Congressional Research Service, Domestic Social Policy Division.

Gomby, D.S., Krantzler, N., Larner, M.B., Stevenson, C.S., Terman, D.L., & Behrman, R.E. (1996). Financing child care: Analysis and recommendations. *The Future of Children, 5*(3), 5–25.

Gustaffson, S., & Stafford, F. (1998). Equity–efficiency tradeoffs and government policy in the United States, the Netherlands, and Sweden. In W.S. Barnett & S.S. Boocock (Eds.), *Early care and education for children in poverty: Promises, programs, and long-term results* (pp. 211–244). Albany, NY: SUNY Press.

Hayes, C., & Danegger, A. (1995). *Rethinking block grants.* Washington, DC: The Finance Project.

Hofferth, S. (1999). Child care, maternal employment, and public policy. *Annals of the American Academy of Political and Social Science, 563,* 20–38.

House Committee on Ways and Means. (1998). *1998 green book: Background material and data on programs within the jurisdiction of the House Committee on Ways and Means.* Washington, DC: U.S. Government Printing Office.

Individuals with Disabilities Education Act Amendments of 1997, PL 105-17, 20 U.S.C. §§ 1400 *et seq.*

Individuals with Disabilities Education Act (IDEA) of 1990, PL 101-476, 20 U.S.C. §§ 1400 *et seq.*

Joint Committee On Taxation. (1998). *Estimates of federal tax expenditures for fiscal years 1999–2003* (Publication No. JCS-7-98). Washington, DC: U.S. Government Printing Office.

Joint Committee On Taxation (2001). *Estimates of federal tax expenditures for fiscal years 2001–2005* (Publication No. JCS-1-01). Washington, DC: U.S. Government Printing Office.

Kimmel, J. (1998). Child care costs as a barrier to employment for single and married mothers. *Review of Economics and Statistics, 80*(2), 287–299.

Kisker, E.E., Hofferth, S.L., Phillips, D.A., & Farquhar, E. (1991). *A profile of child care settings: Early education and care in 1990.* Princeton, NJ: Mathematica Policy Research.

Mitchell, A., Stoney, L., & Dichter, H. (1997). *Financing child care in the United States.* Kansas City, MO: Ewing Marion Kauffman Foundation & Pew Charitable Trusts.

Mitchell, A., Ripple, C., & Chanana, N. (1998). *Prekindergarten programs funded by the states: Essential elements for policy makers.* New York: Families and Work Institute.

Morris, J.R., Helburn, S.W., & Culkin, M.L. (1995). Costs, revenues, and subsidies: A descriptive analysis. In S.W. Helburn (Ed.), *Cost, quality and child outcomes in child care centers: Technical report* (pp. 171–194). Denver: University of Colorado, Department of Economics, Center for Research in Economic Social Policy.

National Association for the Education of Young Children (NAEYC). (1998). *Guide to accreditation by the National Association for the Education of Young Children: 1998 edition.* Washington, DC: Author.

National Center for Education Statistics. (1997). National Household Education

Survey, 1995: Early childhood program participation. In *National Household Education Survey: 1991, 1993, 1995, and 1996 surveys, data files, and electronic codebook.* Washington, DC: U.S. Department of Education.

Office of Management and Budget (OMB). (1999). *Budget of the United States Government: Fiscal year 2000.* Washington, DC: U.S. Government Printing Office.

Office of Management and Budget (OMB). (2001). *Budget of the United States Government: Fiscal year 2002.* Washington, DC: U.S. Government Printing Office.

Office of Management and Budget (OMB). (2002). *Budget of the United States Government: Fiscal year 2003.* Washington, DC: U.S. Government Printing Office.

Olson, L. (2002). Starting early. In Quality counts 2002, *Education Week, 21*(17), 10–14.

Personal Responsibility and Work Opportunity Reconciliation Act of 1996, PL 104-193, 42 U.S.C. §§ 211 *et seq.*

Saluja, G., Early, D.M., & Clifford, R.M. (2002). Demographic characteristics of early childhood teachers and structural elements of early care and education in the United States. *Early Childhood Research and Practice, 4*(1). Retrieved July 29, 2002, from http://ecrp.uiuc.edu/v4n1/saluja.html

Sandham, J.L. (2002). Adequate financing. In Quality counts 2002, *Education Week, 21*(17), 43–45.

Schulman, K., Blank, H., & Ewen, D. (1999). *Seeds of success: State prekindergarten initiatives, 1998–1999.* Washington, DC: Children's Defense Fund.

Schumacher, R. (2002). *Increasing the ability to transfer TANF to CCDF is not the answer to unmet child care needs.* Washington, DC: Center for Law and Social Policy.

St. Pierre, R., Gamse, B., Alamprese, J., Rimdzius, T., & Tao, F. (1998). *National evaluation of the Even Start family literacy program.* Washington, DC: U.S. Department of Education, Planning and Evaluation Service.

Stoney, L., & Greenberg, M.H. (1996). The financing of child care: Current and emerging trends. *The Future of Children, 6*(2), 83–102.

Tietze, W., & Cryer, D. (1999). Current trends in European early child care and education. *Annals of the American Academy of Political and Social Science, 563,* 175–193.

U.S. Bureau of the Census. (2002). *Table PCT12–Sex by age. Universe: Total population* Retrieved August 13, 2002, from http://factfinder.census.gov/servlet/DTTable?ds_name=D&geo_id=D&mt_name=DEC_2000_SF1_U_PCT012&_lang=en

U.S. Department of Agriculture. (2002). *Child and Adult Care Food Program.* Retrieved July 18, 2002, from http://www.fns.usda.gov/pd/ccsummar.htm.

U.S. Department of Education (USDOE). (1992). *Fifteenth annual report to Congress on the implementation of IDEA.* Washington, DC: Author.

U.S. Department of Education (USDOE). (1995). *Seventeenth annual report to Congress on the implementation of IDEA.* Washington, DC: Author.

U.S. Department of Education (USDOE). (1997). *Nineteenth annual report to Congress on the Implementation of IDEA.* Washington, DC: Author.

U.S. Department of Education (USDOE). (1999). *FY 1999 budget summary.* Retrieved June 20, 2002, from http://www.ed.gov/offices/OUS/Budget99/BudgetSum

U.S. Department of Education (USDOE). (2001a). *Twenty-third annual report to Congress on the implementation of IDEA.* Washington, DC: Author.

U.S. Department of Education (USDOE). (2001b). Table 366. Federal on-budget funds obligated for programs administered by the U.S. Department of Education:

Fiscal years 1980 to 2000 [In thousands of dollars]. In *Digest of education statistics, 2001: Federal programs for education and related activities*. Retrieved August 13, 2002, from http://nces.ed.gov/pubs2002/digest2001/tables/dt366.asp

U.S. Department of Health and Human Services (HHS). (1998). *HHS fact sheet: State spending under the Child Care Block Grant*. Washington, DC: U.S. Department of Health and Human Services, Administration for Children and Families.

U.S. Department of Health and Human Services (HHS). (2001). *2001 Head Start fact sheet*. Washington, DC: U.S. Department of Health and Human Services, Administration for Children and Families, Head Start Bureau.

U.S. Department of Health and Human Services (HHS). (2002a). *2002 Head Start fact sheet*. Washington, D.C.: U.S. Department of Health and Human Services, Administration for Children and Families, Administration on Children, Youth and Families, Head Start Bureau.

U.S. Department of Health and Human Services (HHS). (2002b). *2002 welfare fact sheet–Temporary Assistance for Needy Families*. Washington, DC: U.S. Department of Health and Human Services, Administration for Children and Families.

U.S. General Accounting Office (GAO). (1990). *Early childhood education: What are the costs of quality programs?* (Publication No. GAO/HRD-90-43BR). Washington, DC: Author.

U.S. General Accounting Office (GAO). (1994). *Child care subsidies increase likelihood that low-income mothers will work* (Publication No. GAO/HEHS-95-20). Washington, DC: Author.

U.S. General Accounting Office (GAO). (1998). *Child care: Federal funding for fiscal year 1997* (Publication No. GAO/HEHS-98-70R). Washington, DC: Author.

Zill, N., Resnick, G., McKey, R., Clark, C., Connell, D., Swartz, J., O'Brien, R., & D'Elio, M. (1998). *Head Start family and child experiences survey (FACES): Head Start performance measures. Second progress report*. Washington, DC: U.S. Department of Health and Human Services.

Zill, N., & West, J. (2001). *Entering kindergarten: A portrait of American children when they begin school* (Publication No. NCES 2001-035). Washington, DC: U.S. Department of Education, National Center for Education Statistics.

9

Evaluation and Research

Kristin Moore and Jerry West

MECHANISMS FOR EVALUATING EARLY CHILDHOOD EDUCATION AND CARE PROGRAMS AND THEIR EFFECTS

The mechanisms for policy and program evaluation and the bodies that promote data collection and evaluation for early childhood education and care (ECEC) programs in the United States can be conceptualized together. The mechanisms refer to the nature of the data collection effort (evaluative, descriptive, and so forth), and the bodies refer to the agencies supporting the data collection effort. As of 2002, several studies funded by government agencies are collecting information on ECEC.

On one end of the spectrum are program evaluations, which are primarily sponsored by the Administration on Children, Youth and Families (ACYF), which is part of the Administration for Children and Families (ACF) within the U.S. Department of Health and Human Services (DHHS), and by the U.S. Department of Education. Evaluations of programs such as Head Start and Early Head Start are sponsored by ACYF, whereas the evaluation of the Even Start program is sponsored by the U.S. Department of Education. ACF and the Office of the Assistant Secretary for Planning and Evaluation within the DHHS are conducting a number of evaluations of welfare reform, including the National Evaluation of Welfare to Work Strategies and the Child Outcomes at the State Level project.

On the other end of the spectrum are surveys that are nationally representative and descriptive in nature. These can be categorized into repeat cross-sectional and longitudinal studies. The National Center for Education Statistics (NCES), the statistical research division housed within the U.S. Department of Education, sponsors the National Household Education Survey (NHES; 1997), which provides information on a regular basis for tracking participation in ECEC.

NCES also conducts the Early Childhood Longitudinal Study, Kindergarten Class of 1998–99 (ECLS-K), and the Early Childhood Longitudinal Study, Birth Cohort (ECLS-B) These and other longitudinal studies such as the Survey of Income & Program Participation (SIPP; administered by the U.S. Bureau of the Census) and the National Study of Child and Adolescent Well-being (administered by the University of North Carolina, RTI, and ACF), not only provide information on participation in programs but also have the potential to provide evidence of the effects of program participation and experience on children's development and developmental outcomes. The U.S. Department of Labor, Bureau of Labor Statistics, sponsors the National Longitudinal Survey of Youth (NLSY79, NLSY79 Children and Young Adults, and NLSY97). The NLSY studies also provide information on ECEC, though it is retrospective data, except in the case of the NLSY79 Children and Young Adults supplement, which tracks all of the children born to female respondents in biennial interviews.

Other surveys, such as the National Institute of Child Health and Human Development (NICHD) Study of Early Child Care and the Cost, Quality and Child Outcomes (CQO) Study (Helburn, 1995), examine the impact of ECEC on children's growth and development. Data are collected in multiple sites, but the findings cannot be generalized to the nation.

The amount of public funds dedicated to research and program evaluation for ECEC is a complex estimate to produce. For example, funds dedicated to research and program evaluation have been estimated to be about 3% of the total federal research investment of $70 billion (or 6% of the nondefense research and development investment of $31 billion; Executive Office of the President, 1997). (Age-specific data are not available.) The NCES spent 14% of its general statistics budget in fiscal year 1999 on early childhood studies. To our knowledge, the proportion of these monies expended on policy and program evaluation has not been estimated.

CHILD DEVELOPMENT INDICATORS USED IN POLICY DEVELOPMENT AND MONITORING

Commonly Used Indicators

Indicators are measures of children's behavior, development, and attitudes assessed for all children or subgroups of children at a point in time or, especially, over time (Moore, 1997). Indicators cross multiple domains of development, including health and safety, cognitive attainment and educational achievement, and socioemotional development. Measures of families' circumstances are also tracked in most indicator reports.

The measurement of development during the preschool and elementary years is complex and demanding. For young children, straightforward indicator measures, such as whether a teenager has had a baby or has dropped out of high school, are few and far between. The kinds of measures that are appropriate and necessary for young children are difficult and costly to assess for large, nationally representative populations. The ECLS-K and the ECLS-B will provide cognitive, health and safety, and socioemotional measures. The ECLS-K will provide information on a nationally representative sample of children who entered kindergarten in the fall of 1998 and will follow them through their fifth-grade year. The ECLS-B will provide information on a nationally representative sample of children born in the year 2001, and will follow them through their first-grade year. NHES provides additional data collected from parents about children's development and family circumstances in a periodic telephone survey. Other measures come from a variety of data systems, including the vital statistics system and surveys maintained by the National Center for Health Statistics.

The indicators currently tabulated include

- Infant mortality and child mortality, by cause of death
- Birth weight and percentage of births defined as healthy
- General health status of the child, obesity, activity limitations, blood lead levels, dental caries, chronic health conditions
- Child abuse and neglect

- Reading, mathematics, and science proficiency at age 9; difficulty speaking in English; and whether the child was retained in kindergarten or first grade

Other measures that are, strictly speaking, not indicators of child well-being but that capture aspects of the child's background and environment that are strongly linked with children's development are more abundant. Among the measures that are collected and reported are

- Income, poverty, and receipt of public benefits
- Parental labor force participation, maternal employment, and use of child care
- Race, ethnicity, and immigration status
- Residential mobility, housing problems, and residence in low-income neighborhoods
- Family structure, nonmarital births, and the number of children in foster care
- Prenatal care, insurance coverage, and vaccination status
- Seat belt use
- Parent's reading to child, parent–child literacy activities, and parental involvement at grades 3–5
- Enrollment in ECEC programs, including participation in home- and center-based arrangements

Improvements Needed in Early Childhood Education and Care Indicators

Existing indicators of ECEC could be improved in several ways. First, measures that are available at the national level could be made available for states and for substate units, such as cities and counties or school districts. In the United States, many policies for children and families are set by state and local governments, and these agencies need better indicators to inform their work. Reflecting the dearth of state-level data, a foundation-funded survey, the National Survey of America's Families, is being conducted in 13 states. Considerable family information and some indicators for young children are being collected for these 13 states and for the nation.

Second, at all levels, broader arrays of measures are needed for young children. The domains of child well-being, as noted previously, include cognitive attainment and educational achievement, health and safety, and socioemotional development. Even at the national level, these domains are not fully assessed. At the state and local level, there are very substantial gaps, larger in some states and localities than in others, but the gaps are substantial in all states. To collect data that would provide reliable state-level estimates would be very costly. One example of a comprehensive data-gathering effort is the collection of immunization information for preschool children: The Centers for Disease Control and Prevention is conducting a very large telephone survey to assess levels of immunization as reported by parents or guardians.

Third, measures are needed that are seamless across the stages of childhood. Substantial development occurs across the developmental periods of infancy, the toddler years, the preschooler years, and the early elementary school years. Assessments, scales, or observations that score children at all or most of these stages would be helpful to identify when group differences emerge or intensify.

Fourth, information is needed across the domains of development (e.g., cognitive, health and safety, socioemotional) on the *same* child. We need the ability to capture information on multiple risks and family resources in the same surveys that assess the children. For example, presently, understanding the multiple factors that lead to scholastic success or failure is difficult.

Fifth, national indicators of ECEC are based on self-reports of parents and/or program providers. Only the most basic indicators of program quality exist.

THE INFORMATION COLLECTION PROCESS

What information is routinely collected, how the process can be improved, and what areas are identified as major information gaps are related issues. The preponderance of existing national statistics regarding ECEC focuses on participation rates in various environments (e.g., home-based, nonrelative care, Head Start). The surveys that routinely collect information on participation; number of arrangements; and type, frequency, and cost of care are the NHES and the SIPP. These surveys examine care and education from the user's perspective, presenting a picture of the demand for ECEC programs, but they are limited in describing the supply of these programs.

The major information gaps pertain to the ability (or inability) of surveys to provide estimates of the number of programs available nationwide, the types of programs, the characteristics of these programs, and the distribution of characteristics by types of programs (e.g., indicators of quality). Furthermore, from a measurement perspective, basic provider characteristic data collected from parents (which is what is currently available) differ from those collected directly from providers.

How and when this information is collected varies across studies. Many of the larger, nationally representative studies gather information through surveys, often administered over the phone. Several studies, especially those linking ECEC characteristics to child development, employ observation of the care/education environment and direct assessment of children (e.g., self-control tasks). Surveys are conducted periodically, about every 2 years. Studies of child development are generally longitudinal, following the same group of children for the first seven years of their lives, or longer (e.g., NICHD Study of Early Child Care, CQO Study), with follow-ups occurring every 6–12 months. Other surveys have been conducted at only one time (e.g., the National Child Care Survey; Hofferth, Brayfield, Deich, Holcomb, & Glantz, 1990).

Surveys such as the NHES have found that most children in the United States today will receive out-of-home care and/or education before they enter the public school system for kindergarten and that the characteristics of children and families tend to differ by type of ECEC program (e.g., relative, nonrelative, center-based).

In sum, there is considerable information available at the national level, but it is scattered. There is no systematic program designed to provide consistent, comparable, and timely information on ECEC.

USE OF INFORMATION FROM RESEARCH

The data obtained from research on ECEC are used to inform policy and research on the supply and demand of ECEC (see Chapter 3 for further discussion of ECEC supply and demand) and on the impact that this care and education has on children's development. In addition, participant surveys allow estimation of the number of children in ECEC and the type of care/education they are in, whereas provider surveys support estimates of the number of programs available nationwide, the types of programs, and characteristics of programs. Furthermore, staffing studies have informed policies on compensation and reducing turnover (e.g., the military's overhaul of its ECEC system; see Chapter 5). Research is also used to examine the impact of quality of child development to establish a minimum threshold of safety and to describe characteristics that serve to enrich young children's lives; however, there appears to be no fixed threshold because of the mediating child and family characteristics.

Nationally representative studies such as NHES, ECLS-K, and ECLS-B release their data on researcher-friendly CD-ROMs. Typically, the data are released for public use within 1 year of the close of the data collection. Other survey data are made available as well, but the schedule for data release and the form in which data are released varies substantially by survey and by agency. Some databases are 3–5 years old before they are released for secondary analysis.

Although data are available, there is no way to assess the extent to which available indicators are actually used for policy development and monitoring. Reports such as *America's Children: Key National Indicators of Well-Being,* published by the Federal Interagency Forum on Child and Family Statistics; the *KIDS COUNT Data Book,* published annually by The Annie E. Casey Foundation; and *The Condition of Education,* an annual report released by NCES, receive widespread media attention when they are published. This publicity presumably leads the public and policy makers to focus more on these issues, but there is no empirical evidence documenting this. Trends in child poverty and nonmarital childbearing are being monitored to provide evidence regarding the success of the 1996 welfare reform legislation (Personal Responsibility and Work Opportunity Reconciliation Act of 1996, PL 104-193). Also, goals have been set by the U.S. government for health and for education; but there are no incentives attached to meeting the goals, so they serve more as benchmarks for assessing progress.

SUMMARY

In the United States, information from research on brain development has focused attention on the importance of the early years. Increases in maternal employment have led to increased use of child care for infants, toddlers, and preschool children, which has also focused public attention on the child care and education that young children receive. Welfare reform and other public policies have at the same time raised concerns about the development of young children. Yet, relatively little data have become available about children from the time they leave the hospital at birth to when they enter elementary school. However, a number of important, longitudinal national data collection efforts have been initiated, and several important experimental studies have been conducted. Drawing on the knowledge and methods developed in small-scale local studies, the field has been able to move forward remarkably quickly. Nevertheless, gaps in indicators of child well-being, concepts, and measures remain to be addressed.

REFERENCES AND RESOURCES
ON EARLY CHILDHOOD EVALUATION
AND RESEARCH EFFORTS

The Annie E. Casey Foundation. (n.d.). *KIDS COUNT data book* [Published annually]. Available on-line at http://www.aecf.org (click on "Publications" and then click on "KIDS COUNT")

Cost, Quality and Child Outcomes (CQO) Study Team. (1995). *Cost, quality, and child outcomes in child care centers.* Denver: University of Colorado, Center for Research in Economics and Social Policy, Department of Economics.

Executive Office of the President, Office of Science and Technology Policy. (1997, April). *Investing in our future: A national research initiative for America's children for the 21st century.* Washington, DC: Author.

Federal Interagency Forum on Child and Family Statistics. (n.d.). *America's children: Key national indicators of well-being* [Published annually]. Washington, DC: U.S.

Government Printing Office. Also available on-line at http://childstats.gov (click "America's Children: Key National Indicators of Well-Being," then click on "Full Report" or "Full Report in PDF format")

Helburn, S. (Ed.). (1995). *Cost, quality and child outcomes in child care centers: Technical report.* Denver: University of Colorado, Department of Economics, Center for Research in Economic Social Policy.

Hofferth, S.L., Brayfield, A., Deich, S., Holcomb, P., & Glantz, F. (1990). *National Child Care Survey 1990: Parent Study* (AFDA Data Set No. 13–14). Los Altos, CA: Sociometrics.

Moore, K. (1997). Criteria for indicators of child well-being. In R. Hauser, B.V. Brown, & W. Prosser (Eds.), *Indicators of children's well-being* (pp. 36–44). New York: Russell Sage Foundation.

National Center on Education Statistics. (n.d.). *The condition of education* [Published annually]. Available on-line at http://nces.ed.gov/pubsearch/majorpub.asp

National Center on Education Statistics. (n.d.). *Early Childhood Longitudinal Study, Birth Cohort (ECLS-B)* [Study brief]. Retrieved July 9, 2002, from http://nces.ed.gov/ecls/Birth/studybrief.asp

National Center on Education Statistics. (n.d.). *Early Childhood Longitudinal Study, Kindergarten Class of 1998–99 (ECLS-K)* [Study brief]. Retrieved July 9, 2002, from http://nces.ed.gov/ecls/kindergarten/studybrief.asp

National Household Education Survey: 1991, 1993, 1995, and 1996 surveys, data files, and electronic codebook. (1997). Washington, DC: U.S. Department of Education.

National Institute of Child Health and Human Development. (n.d.). *The NICHD Study of Early Child Care* [On-line information about study]. Retrieved July 9, 2002, from http://www.nichd.nih.gov/publications/pubs/early_child_care.htm

Personal Responsibility and Work Opportunity Reconciliation Act of 1996, PL 104-193, 42 U.S.C. §§ 211 *et seq.*

U.S. Bureau of the Census. (n.d.). *Survey of Income & Program Participation (SIPP)* [Survey description; on-line]. Retrieved July 9, 2002, from http://www.census.gov/mp/www/tape/mstap17a.html

U.S. Department of Labor, Bureau of Labor Statistics. (n.d.). *National Longitudinal Surveys home page.* Retrieved July 9, 2002, from http://www.bls.gov/nls/home.htm

10

Innovations in Early Childhood Education and Care

Victoria R. Fu

In the United States, early childhood education and care (ECEC) is embedded in the social, political, and historical context of our nation. Thus, innovations in the field of ECEC are characterized by strong connections among child development, cultural and economic diversity, family–school–community partnership/collaboration, and major social and political influences. The main theme common to innovative endeavors is to facilitate the provision of quality care, education, and other services to young children and their families through professional development and collaboration across systems in multiple contexts. In this chapter, a few of the major innovations in curriculum and practice, teacher preparation, and quality enhancement and improved accessibility are highlighted, followed by a discussion of the influences of evaluation and research on ECEC and the implications of these innovations and research emphases in the early childhood arena.

INNOVATIONS IN CURRICULUM AND PRACTICE

Developmentally Appropriate Practice

The National Association for the Education of Young Children (NAEYC; Bredekamp, 1987; Bredekamp & Copple, 1997) position statements on developmentally appropriate practice (DAP) have been nationally influential in unifying the field of ECEC by articulating the content for teacher education and professional development. Many state departments of education in the United States have adopted these guidelines in making decisions on policy and program evaluation. The strong influence of DAP has also led numerous national organizations to develop their own guidelines and standards that are congruent with these guidelines. More important, the DAP statements have provided a context for dialogue within the field of ECEC and with others outside the field on quality programs for young children and their families. These interactions have influenced the creation of comprehensive, collaborative programs and policies that address the needs of children, youth, and families.

The publication and extensive distribution of DAP opened opportunities for early childhood educators to address the issue of appropriate curriculum and assessment. Furthermore, calls for school reform have raised concerns regarding curriculum content and accountability.

Recognizing a need to link child development knowledge and curriculum theory, NAEYC and the National Association of Early Childhood Specialists in State Departments of Education (NAECS/SDE) published "Guidelines for Appropriate Curriculum Content and Assessment in Programs Serving Children Ages 3 Through 8" (1991). In conjunction with DAP these guidelines have contributed significantly to the establishment of high-quality standards of practice in ECEC. (See Chapter 2 for further discussion of DAP and defining quality in ECEC.)

More recently, at the White House Summit on Early Childhood Cognitive Development (July 27, 2001), it was recognized that the No Child Left Behind Act of 2001 (PL 107-110) could make schools accountable to parents and communities emphasizing the importance of early childhood cognitive development. The summit participants supported the administration's call to develop a science of early childhood development based on research and recommended practices.

The Project Approach

The Project Approach (Katz & Chard, 1989) is an example of an integrated, process-oriented curriculum. The focus of this approach is for children to take on a project that affords in-depth study of a particular topic. The learning process is documented, including children's representation of what they have learned through narratives, drawings, and constructions of artifacts using various media. According to Katz and Chard (1989), the Project Approach to curriculum supports the development of knowledge, skills, and disposition toward learning. Children learn through experimenting and solving problems in cooperation with peers. This approach to teaching and learning has influenced many teachers.

The Reggio Emilia Approach

Many teachers and teacher educators have been inspired by the Reggio Emilia approach to early childhood education, which originated in Italy. The uniqueness of this approach lies in that it presents a collaborative model of ECEC that is based on a social constructivist pedagogy. Schooling is framed in a system of relationships, in which children, teachers, and parents are the three protagonists in this enterprise. The aesthetically and intellectually stimulating environment reflects a respect for the interests, needs, rights, and capabilities of the children and others who occupy that space. Pedagogy is characterized by involving children in projects that encourage in-depth exploration. This approach emphasizes symbolic representation of what is learned, using children's natural languages in their representations. Many ECEC programs are in the process of learning about this approach and adapting it to their respective settings. Some examples include the Jennings Project in Ohio, in which support is provided to teachers to adapt the Reggio Emilia approach in the elementary schools; implementation in lab schools at universities (e.g., Kent State University, University of Vermont, Virginia Polytechnic Institute and State University [Virginia Tech]); middle-school exploration such as that found in Blacksburg, Virginia, in collaboration with Virginia

Tech; and many private and public ECEC centers across the nation (discussed later in this chapter). Horm-Wingerd (2002) addressed issues related to standards, comprehensive measures of learning, and accountability assessment in the United States, from an inquiry-based perspective, with lessons learned from Reggio Emilia.

INNOVATIONS IN TEACHER PREPARATION

Bachelor's and Advanced Degrees

Variability is found across professional preparation, in spite of the availability of approved standards for teacher preparation for 4- and 5-year institutions by the National Council for Accreditation of Teacher Education (NCATE) and NAEYC, which is an affiliate member of NCATE. This inconsistency is due mainly to the fact that much early childhood teacher preparation continues to be influenced by state certification standards, many of which do not focus on early childhood. However, the NAEYC publications *A Conceptual Framework for Early Childhood Professional Development* (1993) and *Guidelines for Preparation of Early Childhood Professionals* (1996) have encouraged teacher preparation programs to develop a coherent, conceptual framework that reflects the knowledge base of the field. Educational reform movement has provided the impetus for teacher education and subject-discipline organizations to work together to improve professional preparation and training. For example, the National Institute for Early Childhood Professional Development, a division of NAEYC, has established a program review system at the baccalaureate and advanced levels at institutions of higher education that seek accreditation from NCATE.

Associate Degrees and Articulation of Agreements Between 2- and 4-Year Programs

The National Institute for Early Childhood Professional Development is currently developing an early childhood education program approval system for associate degree professional preparation programs (2-year teacher education programs). American Associate Degree Early Childhood Educators (ACCESS), the national community college organization for early childhood teacher educators, is working with NAEYC and NCATE in this effort. This initiative opens up opportunities for partnerships in teacher education that may lead to more effective preparation of qualified teachers to teach in diverse ECEC environments. This effort also can facilitate articulation of agreements between 2- and 4-year programs to prepare a larger number of qualified teachers to meet a shortage in our country. Connecticut, for example, has initiated an Early Childhood Articulation Plan. Under this plan, colleges and universities in the state have developed an articulation plan so that graduates with associate degrees may enter baccalaureate teacher certification programs without losing time and credits.

Child Development Associate Credential

The Council for Professional Recognition, funded by the federal government, administers the Child Development Associate (CDA) program—a performance-based program that assesses and provides credentials for ECEC professionals. The trend is for community colleges to offer the equivalent of 2 years of college education to CDA candidates. In addition to being required for employment in Head Start, the CDA credential has become a part of regulations for licensing ECEC programs in many states. (See Chapter 5 for further discussion of the CDA credential.)

Constructivist Teacher Preparation Programs

There is growing interest in the field of ECEC on constructivism and its relevance in curriculum, practice, teacher education, and school reform. Broadly speaking, this integrated, inquiry-based approach to teacher education is influenced by the works of Piaget, Vygotsky, and Dewey, among others. This framework of teacher preparation is in line with the guidelines and philosophy of DAP in multiple contexts in which development occurs and reflects the standards and position statements of leading councils and commissions of teacher education organization in science, mathematics, social studies, and art. Learning is considered to be both process and product, and young children's learning is represented through symbolic representation. Reggio Emilia has much to contribute to the constructivist approach to teacher preparation.

Teacher Preparation
Programs Inspired by Reggio Emilia

As discussed previously, a trend toward inquiry based, constructivist approach to early childhood teacher education inspired by the Reggio Emilia approach is growing in the United States. This has led to a need to reconstruct the Reggio Emilia approach to inform teaching in the context of the United States. Teacher education programs that include elements of the Reggio Emilia Approach include Kent State University, Ohio State University, University of New Hampshire, University of Tennessee, the University of Vermont, and Virginia Tech. For example, the Virginia Tech teacher preparation program is based on inquiry and social constructivism; is informed by the philosophy and theories of Dewey, Piaget, Vygotsky, Gardner, and others; and is inspired by the Reggio Emilia approach. The Virginia Tech Child Development Lab School embraces a negotiated curriculum that is child initiated and teacher framed. The notions of teacher as researcher and collaborative inquiry permeate its teacher education courses and field and student teaching experiences. Documentation is an integral part of the teacher education program as it promotes reflection on curriculum, practice, child development, family involvement, and diversity issues and the personal, professional development of the student teachers.

INNOVATIONS IN EARLY
CHILDHOOD EDUCATION AND CARE
QUALITY ENHANCEMENT AND ACCESSIBILITY

National Education Goals Panel

The now-defunct National Education Goals Panel, a bipartisan and intergovernmental body established in 1990, defined eight national goals to "help provide a national framework for education reform and promote systemic changes needed to ensure equitable educational opportunities and high levels of educational achievement for all students." Goal 1, named "Ready to Learn," which appeared in the Goals 2000: Educate America Act of 1994 (PL 103-227), established an objective that by 2000 all children would have had access to high-quality, developmentally appropriate programs. This panel also promoted and monitored the progress toward the goals and supported systemwide reform, including the following: establishing a system of high academic standards and assessments; identifying actions for federal, state, and local governments; and building a nationwide, bipartisan consensus to achieve the goals.

Accreditation by the National Association for the Education of Young Children

The National Academy of Early Childhood Programs, the accreditation department of NAEYC, has established standards for accreditation of quality early childhood programs. The third edition of this accreditation system (NAEYC, 1998) is widely recognized for ECEC programs in centers, schools, and many other settings that serve children and their families. Criteria of accreditation have served as "benchmarks for other standard-setting bodies, funders, and professional development programs" (p. v) in the United States and internationally (cf. Chapter 8 for a different perspective on NAEYC accreditation standards).

Public–Private Partnerships

There are many efforts to create and maintain public–private partnerships for ECEC across the United States. Establishing partnerships for ECEC is fast becoming a way to draw together resources and knowledge to improve quality and increase supply and accessibility of ECEC in communities across the United States. One project that warrants special attention is the Child Care Partnership Project, supported by the U.S. Department of Health and Human Services, Administration for Children and Families, the Administration on

Children, Youth and Families, and the Child Care Bureau. In addition to working toward the partnership goals just mentioned, the programs in the Child Care Partnership Project also provide technical assistance on work–life issues and raise revenue to build and improve state and community ECEC systems. The Child Care Partnership Project profiles more than two dozen public–private partnership models as examples of successful programs. The following are a few examples of programs that have demonstrated sustainability, a history of broad based support, and a strong evaluation component and have achieved national renown:

- *Georgia Voluntary Prekindergarten Program:* Georgia has a statewide program of universal preschool. The mission of this program of for all 4-year-olds is to prepare children for school. This collaborative program is administered by the Office of School Readiness (OSR), and staff report directly to the governor. Programs usually operate on the public school calendar. To maintain high quality, the curriculum of the participating programs is approved by OSR, and services, such as reduced-fee meals, subsidies for before- and after-school care, resource coordination, and other services are provided for children at risk. Parent involvement, a high priority of the program, is encouraged through a range of activities that extend children's learning at home through parent education and through life-skills classes. This initiative has been recognized nationally as a model for replication.

- *North Carolina Partnership for Children (Smart Start):* The North Carolina Partnership for Children (NCPC) initiative supports county-level Smart Start partnerships with funding, technical assistance on program development, administration, organizational development, communications, fiscal management, technology, contracts management, and fundraising. The NCPC also sets statewide goals for early childhood programs and services. All children from birth to age 5 and their families are eligible for Smart Start services, regardless of income. Smart Start has been widely recognized as a comprehensive model for early childhood initiatives for national, state, and local policy discussions and adaptation.

- *T.E.A.C.H. (Teacher Education and Compensation Helps) Early Childhood Project:* The focus of the T.E.A.C.H. Early Childhood Project is to improve the training of child care workers, and additional training is linked to higher wages. "By compensating child care workers for receiving more training and education, the program works to retain child care providers and improve the quality of the child care workforce" (National Child Care Information Center, n.d.) The multi-state initiative, which was started in North Carolina by Day Care Services Association, is a nonprofit service, research, and advocacy group. To replicate this model, states must apply to Day Care Services Association for a license and meet the following requirements: 1) Each state must use the educational system in place to provide training; 2) the diversity of the workforce, including the providers' different educational levels, geographic locations (urban and rural), and settings for the care they provide (center-based and home care options) must be respected; and 3) the project must receive payment from public and private partners involved in the program. The project has a built-in evaluation component to track progress toward the goal. It has been adopted by other states, including New York, Pennsylvania, Georgia, Florida, Colorado, and Indiana. (See Chapter 5 for further discussion of the T.E.A.C.H. Early Childhood Project.)

Head Start and Early Head Start

For the 1994 Head Start reauthorization legislation and in response to the changing needs of children, families, and communities, a bipartisan advisory committee was formed to review the Head Start program and make recommendations for both expansion and improvements. In *Creating a 21st Century Head Start: Final Report of the Advisory Committee on Head Start Quality and Expansion* (U.S. Department of Health and Human Services, 1993), the committee recommended improving staff training and career development, including better salaries for Head Start workers; improving management of local Head Start centers; reengineering federal oversight; and providing better facilities. Bipartisan legislation (the Head Start Reauthorization Act of 1994, PL 103-252) was passed to reauthorize and strengthen the Head Start program. This legislation also established Early Head Start, a program for low-income pregnant women and families with infants and toddlers. As with Head Start, Early Head Start focuses on the "four cornerstones essential to quality programs: child development, family development, community building and staff development" (U.S. Department of Health and Human Services, Administration for Children and Families, n.d.-b). The U.S. Department of Health and Human Services, Administration for Children and Families (n.d.-a) provides information regarding Head Start performance standards and other regulations. The Head Start Family and Child Experiences Survey (FACES), a national longitudinal study of the cognitive, social, emotional development of children in Head Start, was initiated in 1997. A battery of observation and assessment instruments were developed for this survey. The Advisory Committee on Head Start Research and Evaluation (n.d.) publishes findings and the FACES instruments.

INFLUENCES OF RESEARCH, ASSESSMENT, AND EVALUATION

There is an increasing move toward quality enhancement through the establishment and implementation of standards for teacher preparation, program evaluation, and research. Successful programs, such as those mentioned previously, have purposefully built-in research, assessment, and evaluation components. The following are some other examples of research and evaluation initiatives.

Literacy

According to researchers at the Center for the Improvement of Early Reading Achievement, there is a need for research that attends to the sociocultural and biographical contexts in literacy acquisition. This is because the foundation of children's literacy begins at home in family literacy practices and depends, in part, on parents' knowledge, skills, and motivation for reading and, in part, on the ways that parents and teachers provide mutually reinforcing instruction to children

(Dickinson & Tabors, 2001). One more example of the impact of research on education is in the area of development of literacy in young children. The International Reading Association (IRA) and NAEYC (1998) developed a joint position statement on early literacy development. This statement is based on research on young children's literacy development and current issues related to this topic.

One of the programs that holds promise to enhance the acquisition in literacy skills is the Even Start Family Literacy Program. This program helps parents of educationally disadvantaged children ages 1–7 years to become partners in their children's education through grants to schools for family-centered education. This program takes an integrated, intergenerational approach to serve young children and their parents through cooperative projects with communities.

Research on Early Brain Development

The implications of research on child development have had substantial impact on educational policy and practices. For example, the Regional Educational Laboratories and the Education Commission of the States, among other leadership organizations, have called for the exploration of the implications of neuroscience research for early childhood education, child care, teacher preparation, special education, parental engagement, and prevention programs.

Head Start and Early Head Start Research and Evaluation

Research and evaluation for accountability and quality improvement play an increasingly significant role in the federally funded Head Start and Early Head Start. Four Head Start Quality Research Centers have been established to study the effects of Head Start on children and families over time, collaborating with the National Academy of Sciences and the National Institutes of Health. Another effort to build linkages between research, practice, and policy is through the annual Head Start National Research Conference, which serves as a forum for sharing information and building partnerships across disciplines.

IMPLICATIONS FOR THE
UNITED STATES AND OTHER COUNTRIES

The following are a few reflections on the innovations in ECEC that are described in this chapter and their national and international implications:

- Programs and issues in ECEC should be examined and under-stood contextually. That is, there is a need to take into account the social, cultural, economic, political, historical, and current contexts.

- Development and revision of guidelines for appropriate curricu-lum and practice and for teacher education and professional devel-opment standards across ECEC calls for collaboration among pro-fessional organizations and across disciplines.

- Education of qualified ECEC teachers is the shared responsibility of 2-year, 4-year, and advanced degree–granting institutions of higher education. There is a need for these institutions to collabo-rate to articulate teacher education plans that facilitate professional development and movement from beginning to advanced levels of education.

- Collaborative private and public partnerships with strong leader-ship and administration—nationally, statewide, and locally—have the potential to make quality, affordable care and education acces-sible to all children and families and to improve compensation for professionals in ECEC.

- Innovations call for openness to practices and approaches that can be learned from diverse programs in the United States and inter-nationally.

- Research in diverse fields such as child development and neuro-science can contribute significantly to improving the education, care, and services for children and their families.

- Research, assessment, and evaluation are essential to program enhancement; accountability; and the building of knowledge about child development curricula, recommended practice, and ECEC policy.

REFERENCES

Advisory Committee on Head Start Research and Evaluation. (n.d.). *Head Start Family and Child Experiences Survey (FACES)*. Retrieved August 12, 2002, from http://www2.acf.dhhs.gov/programs/hsb/hsreac/faces/index.html

Bredekamp, S. (1987). *Developmentally appropriate practice in early childhood programs serving children from birth through age 8*. Washington, DC: National Association for the Education of Young Children.

Bredekamp, S., & Copple, C. (Eds.). (1997). *Developmentally appropriate practice in early childhood programs* (Rev. ed.). Washington, DC: National Association for the Education of Young Children.

Dickinson, D.K., & Tabors, P.O. (Eds.). (2001). *Beginning literacy with language: Young children learning at home and school*. Baltimore: Paul H. Brookes Publishing Co.

Goals 2000: Educate America Act of 1994, PL 103-227, 20 U.S.C. §§ 5801 *et seq.*

Head Start Reauthorization Act of 1994, PL 103-252, 42 U.S.C. §§ 9831 *et seq.*

Horm-Wingerd, D. (2002). The Reggio Emilia approach and accountability assessment in the United States. In V.R. Fu, A.J. Stremmel, & L.T. Hill (Eds.), *Teaching and learning: Collaborative exploration of the Reggio Emilia approach* (pp. 51–65). Upper Saddle River, NJ: Merrill/Prentice-Hall.

International Reading Association (IRA) & National Association for the Education for Young Children (NAEYC). (1998, July). Learning to read and write: Developmentally appropriate practices for young children. A joint position statement of the International Reading Association (IRA) and the National Association for the Education for Young Children (NAEYC). *Young Children, 53*(4), 30–46.

Katz, L.G., & Chard, S.C. (1989). *Engaging children's minds: The Project Approach*. Stamford, CT: Ablex.

National Association for the Education of Young Children (NAEYC). (1993). *A conceptual framework for early childhood professional development*. Washington, DC: Author.

National Association for the Education of Young Children (NAEYC). (1996). *Guidelines for preparation of early childhood professionals*. Washington, DC: Author.

National Association for the Education of Young Children (NAEYC) & National Association of Early Childhood Specialist in State Departments of Education (NAECS/SDE). (1991, March). Guidelines for appropriate curriculum content and assessment in programs serving children ages 3 through 8. *Young Children,* 21–38.

National Education Goals Panel. (n.d.). *NEGP: Goals* [On-line]. Retrieved July 9, 2002, from http://www.negp.gov/page3.htm

National Child Care Information Center. (n.d.) *T.E.A.C.H. Early Childhood Project*. Retrieved July 9, 2002, from http://www.nccic.org/ccpartnerships/profiles/teach.htm

No Child Left Behind Act of 2001, PL 107-110, 20 U.S.C.

U.S. Department of Health and Human Services. (1993, December). *Creating a 21st century Head Start: Final report of the Advisory Committee on Head Start Quality and Expansion*. Washington, DC: Author. Also available on-line at http://www.bmcc.org/Headstart/21Century/

U.S. Department of Health and Human Services, Administration for Children and Families. (n.d.-a). *Head Start Bureau: Program performance standards and other regulations.* Retrieved August 12, 2002, from http://www.acf.hhs.gov/programs/hsb/performance/index.htm

U.S. Department of Health and Human Services, Administration for Children and Families. (n.d.-b). *Region III: Philadelphia. Head Start programs.* Retrieved August 12, 2002, from http://www.acf.dhhs.gov/programs/region3/r3hstart.htm

11

Challenges for Early Childhood Education and Care Policy

Richard M. Clifford,
Moncrieff Cochran, and Sharon Lynn Kagan

Early childhood education and care (ECEC) is defined broadly in this book to include care and education provided by parents and other relatives as well as by others in settings outside the child's home. Within this overall framework, changes in ECEC policy have come within three separate but complementary movements: primary prevention, child care, and family support. Primary prevention has its roots in the 1960s discovery of childhood poverty and its consequences, which led to establishment of the federal Head Start program. Modern manifestations are found not only in Head Start but also in a myriad of national, state, and local home visiting programs, aimed primarily at the needs of children from birth to 3 years old and their families. The modern child care movement was stimulated by the entry of millions of mothers into the work force during the early 1970s, a shift that has continued unabated and been given further impetus by federal and state welfare reform. The family support movement began in local communities as a reaction to the deficit-oriented, individualistic character of prevailing parent education and family assistance programs and gained prominence in the early 1980s with formation of the Family Resource Coalition of America. The 1990s were a time of great vibrancy and growing excitement, involving unprecedented growth within all three of these early care and education streams and some indication that the currents were beginning to intermingle and nourish one another. At the same time, this vibrancy brought with it increased complexity, in part because many policy makers continue to address the three arenas separately. This complexity has led to confusion and frustration in many local communities.

SIGNIFICANT SHIFTS INFLUENCING EARLY CHILDHOOD EDUCATION AND CARE POLICY

Some of the most important societal shifts that have influenced ECEC policy are summarized in the sections that follow. An emphasis is given to child care and early childhood education policy, but many of the changes are also manifested in family support and primary prevention policies.

More Sophisticated Understanding of the Links Between Policy and Program Quality

A shift toward greater understanding of the ways in which policy and quality are interconnected is well represented in research. Studies since the early 1990s have moved from a focus on the general impacts of ECEC programs on child growth and development to an increased emphasis on whether, and how, programs of differing quality have differential effects on that development. This greater attention to specific quality indicators such as the education and training of ECEC teachers/caregivers, staff turnover rates, staff–child ratios, and the closeness of the teacher–child relationship has begun to be translated into national, state, and local policy initiatives aimed specifically at improving those program dimensions. Somewhat analogous shifts in the direction of specifying key dimensions and promising practices have been seen in the family support and home visiting arenas.

Increased National Dialogue About
What Constitutes Quality Education and Care

The guidelines for developmentally appropriate practice (Bredekamp, 1987), published in 1987 by the National Association for the Education of Young Children (NAEYC) and revised in 1997 (Bredekamp & Copple, 1997), and the intervening decade of discussions and debate (see Chapters 2 and 10) have led to growing consensus in the ECEC field regarding the nature and dynamics of high-quality group care for young children. Challenges to the values and pedagogy framing developmentally appropriate practice have contributed to an understanding of its limitations and allowed culturally appropriate alternatives to take shape. Another milestone was reached with the introduction of the Anti-Bias Curriculum (Derman-Sparks & ABC Task Force) in 1989, which provided practitioners with ways of understanding the negative effects of racism, sexism, and handicappism on early development. This work has become the accepted guide to teaching methods that empower children regardless of ability, gender, or cultural background. More recently, the work of California Tomorrow has moved the discussion of how to develop culturally appropriate preschool programs beyond curriculum to include hiring practices, family–center relations, and language differences.

Increased recognition of the central role played by teacher education and training in the provision of high-quality care has brought acknowledgment of the fact that there has been no system for developing well-trained practitioners in ECEC in the United States and is leading to more focused efforts by states to create such systems (see Chapter 5). These efforts are still in the early stages. Community colleges are poised to play a central role in the systems that emerge from these efforts (see Chapter 10).

Growing Recognition of Higher
Center Standards on a National Scale

The introduction of a voluntary center-based program accreditation system by NAEYC in 1985 set a quality standard substantially higher than those reflected in the minimal health and safety regulations provided by the states. Since then, this standard (which was revised in 1991 and 1998) has come to be recognized and adopted by thousands of programs, a growing number of states, and several for-profit child care corporations. State regulations (see Chapter 4) governing center-based ECEC also became somewhat more stringent during the 1990s, especially regarding staff–child ratios for infant care (Azer, LeMoine, Morgan, Clifford, & Crawford, 2002).

Greater Attention to the Economics of Early Childhood Education and Care

The 1990s saw greatly intensified efforts to understand the full cost of providing quality ECEC programs and renewed efforts to broaden the funding base beyond parents to include the public and private sectors. The federal expenditure of public funds has increased dramatically, as have state tax expenditures. By the year 2000, 42 states were investing tax funds in prekindergarten programs alone, not counting investments in child care and related ECEC programs (Schulman, Blank, & Ewen, 1999; see also Chapter 8). A number of states have reinvested some of the savings accrued through welfare reform in child care for low-income families—such as through the transfer of Temporary Assistance for Needy Families funds to the Child Care and Development Fund allowable under federal regulations. Child care tax credits for parents and tax deductions for employers providing or subsidizing child care services have expanded at both federal and state levels. Lower income families benefit the least from these tax-based strategies and generally pay a far higher percentage of family income for child care than do wealthier families (see Chapter 8).

New strategies have been developed for linking financing to quality, including federal requirements setting aside specific percentages of federal funds for investment in quality improvement through teacher education, improved adult–child ratios, and other such approaches. States have also begun to develop tiered reimbursement plans with higher quality programs qualifying for higher reimbursement rates. Teacher compensation is increasingly linked to amount and type of education and training completed by teachers (see Chapter 5), and the percentage of certified teachers hired by centers is in turn related to subsidy rates. Concerted national efforts are underway within the private nonprofit sector to increase the salaries of child care providers and early childhood education teachers.

The for-profit child care sector has continued to expand since the mid-1980s, especially in states with less stringent child care center regulations regarding staff–child ratio and teacher qualifications.

Expanded State Involvement in Early Childhood Education and Care

The 1990s brought substantially increased state involvement in ECEC, partly because of pressures for decentralization at the federal level and partly because states are recognizing the value of primary prevention, early education, and family support as front-end investments with long-term savings. These investments have been especially evident in prekindergarten programs for 3- and 4-year-olds (Schulman et al., 1999) but are also seen in home-visiting programs for families with infants and toddlers, early developmental screening, and programming for children with special needs. In some cases, as with welfare reform, the change has not involved increased expenditure of state tax revenues but rather reallocation of federal funds allocated to states through block grants (see Chapter 1). There are growing signs that the role of public schools is expanding to include services for younger children in a more comprehensive array of services to families. By the late 1990s, nearly 1 million children younger than the standard entry age for school were in school-based programs (Clifford, Early, & Hills, 1999).

Increased Emphasis on Primary Prevention

The greater appreciation of the value of primary prevention mentioned earlier can be seen in changes within the federal Head Start program to include substantial investment in programming for children from birth to 3 years old and their families (Early Head Start). Recognition of the importance of the parent role in infant care is reflected in passage of federal parental leave legislation, the Family and Medical Leave Act (FMLA) of 1993 (PL 103-3; discussed in Chapter 7), although the absence of any salary replacement seriously limits its usefulness to lower and middle-income families. Many of the child care initiatives flowing from welfare reform are also aimed at the needs of parents with very young children. The growing interest in primary prevention is also reflected in the health-oriented home visiting programs and policies on early screening for disabilities that were mentioned earlier.

Growing Recognition of the Need for a Systemic Approach and Greater Coordination

A major shortcoming for ECEC in the United States has been the absence of comprehensive, coherent infrastructures at the federal, state, or local levels to support ECEC programming. Several important national reports (e.g., *Not by Chance: Creating an Early Care and Education System for America's Children,* Kagan & Cohen, 1997) have highlighted the need for systems of ECEC at every level and for comprehensive planning and long-range thinking. During the 1990s, the expansion of private, nonprofit child care resource and referral (CCR&R) agencies at the local level brought more coherence and coordination to local ECEC efforts for planners, providers, and parents. In addition, at the state level, numerous commissions have been given authority to plan for a comprehensive system of ECEC. Often these state-level entities are linked with local councils or commissions so that decision-making is devolved and better coordinated. At the national level and in some states, associations of CCR&R agencies have become effective advocates for increased public funding and other enhancements to the overall ECEC effort.

Resurgence of Attention to Kith and Kin Care

Since the passage of the federal welfare reform law, the Personal Responsibility and Work Opportunity Reconciliation Act of 1996 (PL 104-193), attention has shifted once more to early childhood care provided by kith and kin (close friends and family members). This shift was stimulated by the requirement in PL 104-193 that parents be able to choose among available child care providers, including their own relatives and neighbors. Increased amounts of public funds are going to kith and kin, who are exempt from state regulations because they care for only one or two children or provide care for only a few hours per day. Renewed policy efforts are also underway in some states to find effective ways of supporting and enhancing the efforts of these caregivers through home visiting and other family support strategies. There is concern, however, about the overall level of quality available in these largely unregulated settings.

Growing Recognition of the Need for Consumer Education

There is growing recognition that continued expansion of the resources allocated to ECEC in the United States depends on increased demand for such expenditures by the voting public. Increase in this demand will require education of that public about the benefits flowing from such increased investment and the costs of not investing more. The first major national effort to provide education information using a variety of media was carried out in the mid-1990s and focused on findings in brain research and implications of those findings for ECEC. Since then, the relationship between the quality of ECEC and school performance, especially children's success in reading by third grade, has dominated the public debate.

Changes in the Context Surrounding Early Childhood Education and Care

The shifts outlined thus far represent progress in the direction of improved ECEC systems at all levels and a clear increase in the rate of that progress during the 1990s. But these positive changes must be understood in the context of daunting demographic changes in the United States as a whole and especially as they relate to ECEC teachers. Demographic shifts in the U.S. population involve increases in the percent of children from families whose historical origins are not European and whose home language is not English. Laws requiring that only English be spoken in early childhood programs receiving public funds are becoming increasingly common in the states. The salaries of ECEC teachers, already very low (see Chapter 5 for specific statistics from the U.S. Department of Labor, Bureau of Labor Statistics), actually declined in purchasing power during the 1990s. A shortage of qualified ECEC teachers already exists and is expected to have worsened dramatically by 2010. Shortages of infant and toddler caregivers and programs are especially acute, and the quality of existing programs is alarming low. All these realities argue for quickening the pace of ECEC policy advancement over the next decade.

ADAPTATION OF EARLY CHILDHOOD EDUCATION AND CARE SYSTEMS AND PRACTICES TO SHIFTS IN THE POLICY ENVIRONMENT

The dissemination of innovations in the United States is seriously impeded by the decentralized nature of our system. The result is great variation from state to state and even within states. In general, federal, state, and local efforts continue to attempt to articulate with one another, although this is difficult. In a given state, much depends on local capacity to plan and coordinate ECEC programs as well as the level of commitment to ECEC at the state level. Political attitudes in state governments affect the extent to which states are even willing to take advantage of financing allocations and incentives offered by the federal government. Advocacy at federal, state, and local levels has become increasingly sophisticated and has some impact in influencing systems change. In short, there is great variation in the way states and communities react to the shifts discussed previously.

POLICY QUESTIONS FOR THE FUTURE

The shifts in factors influencing the early childhood field discussed previously are evidenced increasingly in current policies. However, there is a set of policy concerns critical to the further advancement of

ECEC in the United States that deserves ongoing attention. These major policy issues relate to the establishment of a comprehensive system of services for young children and their families. Four general questions can be asked in regard to policy considerations: Who will provide early childhood services in this country? Who will teach and care for our youngest citizens? Who will pay for early childhood services? Who will govern these services? Each is discussed in the following sections.

Who Will Provide Early Childhood Services?

The provision of early childhood services in the United States has been compared with parallel play in young children. The United States has a variety of providers of services, each operating in their own way with little coordination or even communication across the segments of the provider community. As described previously, Head Start programs, federally supported and governed, serve nearly 1 million young children, mostly 3 and 4 years of age. U.S. public school systems, mostly under the control of some 17,000 local school boards, serve nearly 1 million children as well (Clifford et al., 1999). The U.S. child care network of some 100,000 centers and an even larger number of family child care homes is composed of private for-profit providers (including some that are parts of large chains, but most are operated as small businesses), nonprofit agencies (mostly controlled by local boards of directors), and public agencies (including schools, hospitals, and other governmental entities), together serving millions of additional children. Layered on top of these primary providers is a set of services for young children with disabilities or developmental risk and their families. Often these services are provided in one of the settings just described but paid for by public dollars through a separate funding stream. In many locations, however, services are also available through specialized early intervention programs in segregated settings.

Each of these groups of service providers operates relatively independently with no overarching mechanism for coordination and control. Although the segments act independently, the actions of one segment often have a profound impact on the others. When the public school system in a community or state makes a decision to radically expand services to 4-year-old children, this may be seen by the private for-profit child care providers or by the local Head Start program as unfair competition. Similarly, expansion of Head Start to serve younger children (e.g., by adding an Early Head Start component to serve infants and toddlers) may affect the early intervention services in the community and may also take customers from the local child care centers and family child care providers.

Research is expanding our understandings of differences in the nature and quality of services offered by various sectors, but still much more needs to be known: How many children are actually served by the various sectors of the service provider community, and how are these numbers changing over time? Do the advantages in quality offered by the public sector justify the higher cost of these programs? Are there mechanisms for successfully coordinating the existing set of services? To what degree do existing government policies act to constrain quality in favor of providing services to a larger number of children and families? What infrastructure supports are necessary to enhance quality in the entire system? In general, how has the substantial increase in government funding for early childhood services affected the nature and quality of services since the early 1990s?

Who Will Teach and Care for Young Children?

As described previously, there is wide variation across the United States in who serves as the primary caregiver/teacher of young children. There is evidence that more highly educated professionals offer higher quality services, which lead to better outcomes in children. There is also evidence that child–staff ratios are at least as important in providing quality. In other countries, however, there is evidence that high-quality services can be achieved by employing well-trained teachers with relatively large child–staff ratios. Studies are needed to determine the best ways of improving quality of services at reasonable costs. Decisions about who will work with young children are also political in nature, so studies must look at the impact of a variety of methods of achieving quality. Infant care is a particular case.

With no government-mandated paid parental leave, more than half of all women return to work within 1 year of having a child. Studies of child care indicate that the quality of services for infants is a major problem in the United States. Is it more economical for the government to support some form of parental leave or to support high-quality infant care? What are the relative advantages to the families and to the children themselves? It should be noted that national commissions and panels have been addressing this question. For example, the National Research Council's report *Eager to Learn: Educating our Preschoolers* (Bowman, Donovan, & Burns, 2001) made provocative recommendations regarding the credentialing of workers in the field.

Who Will Pay for Early Childhood Services?

The United States still relies on parents to pay for the largest part of the cost of ECEC. The United States has a complex system of both direct and indirect methods for providing government support for families using these services at the state and federal levels. In some cases, the costs are fully borne by the government, as in Head Start and many public school–based programs. Child care subsidies are available for lower income families through federal and state programs usually administered by local social service agencies. These subsidies often require some family co-payment except for families with very low incomes. Tax credits are available for most families using child care to permit parents to work. There have been quite substantial increases in government investment in ECEC since the early 1990s. We are beginning to discern the impact of financing methods on the quality of services. Although certain methods of providing support are thought to encourage use of lower cost and lower quality settings, far more research is needed to understand the cost and quality relationships and to guide public policy making in this area. Important work is being launched in this area, and it should provide critical information to guide policy. For example, studies are underway to determine the true cost of quality services, suitable financing models from other fields, and inventive approaches to finance ECEC.

Who Will Govern Early
Childhood Education and Care?

Although the issue of who should govern ECEC in the United States is not one that will require extensive research, decisions about the roles of the federal, state, and local governments will have a profound impact on the nature, quality, and delivery of services. The United States is in dire need of a consensus about the relative roles of these different parts of the governance structure, about who should be empowered to govern (e.g., elected representatives or appointed individuals), and about the standardization of functions among governance structures, given the movement toward policy devolution. Although decisions are being etched out at the local and state levels, some experts have called for a national commission to openly discuss and debate these issues.

ADDITIONAL ISSUES FOR THE FUTURE

Three other areas of concern deserve special mention in this discussion: determining the role of family support, gaining insights from brain research, and making ECEC responsive to diversity.

What Is the Role of the
Broader Concept of Family Support?

Research on the efficacy of family support in the United States is equivocal. For example, studies of home visiting offer only limited support for these programs' ability to substantially impact family functioning. Yet many European countries offer some forms of broader family support. The studies of U.S. family support use limited measures of the impact of such supports for families that may not capture the true value of such services. Although more research is needed in this area, feedback from parents and families attests to the value of family support services.

How Can We Make Early Childhood Education and Care Responsive to the Needs of the Increasingly Diverse Population?

As mentioned in Chapters 5 and 6, the population of young children is rapidly becoming more diverse. Programs are dealing with making accommodations for families with limited proficiency in the English language and with understanding and building on the rich diversity of cultures. Open discussion of the issues related to this growing diversity is needed to take advantage of what is already known about working with diverse groups, and identification of new avenues of investigation is needed to move thinking in the field forward.

One particular issue is the degree to which teachers are representative of the population of children served. Although public schools have had a hard time providing a teacher work force that is as diverse as its student population, there is some hope that the early childhood work force is more diverse (Saluja, Early, & Clifford, 2001). But efforts to professionalize the early childhood workforce by requiring higher levels of training may have the unintended effect of decreasing the cultural and ethnic diversity of teachers. Specific efforts to ensure that the teaching work force remain diverse will be needed.

ANTICIPATED TRENDS IN FUTURE POLICY DEVELOPMENT

ECEC in the United States has experienced a period of profound change since the 1960s and especially since the early 1990s. The mid-1960s gave rise to sustained formal federal intervention (via Head Start and the Elementary and Secondary Education Act of 1965 [PL 89-10]) for the first time in the nation's history. Since then, remarkable though insufficient increases in federal and state supports along with a growth in the number of unconnected programs and services have characterized the epoch. Given the absence of an infrastructure on which to build such efforts systematically and the advent of devolution, both the federal government and the states are experiencing systemic inadequacies which, of necessity, will frame major efforts in the future. Thus, recent explosive growth within the ECEC field coupled with significant demographic and technological changes outside the field predict that the coming decades will be a time of both unprecedented opportunity and challenge for ECEC. With the shifts influencing the ECEC field and with the questions just discussed in mind, we anticipate the following trends.

Quality

As study after study has indicated, American policy efforts since the 1970s have focused on the expansion of the *quantity* of services, rather than their *quality*. This is the single most serious challenge facing the ECEC field, for several reasons. First, tackling quality in a nation as diverse as the United States means that no single regulatory or curricular strategy can be universally applied. Regulations, if they are to be made more stringent, will need to be handled on a state-by-state basis. The recruitment and training of professionals is, similarly, a state responsibility. Second, there is no agreed-on definition of quality (see Chapter 2) or national value set on which to base a quality improvement movement. Ideas about what constitutes quality, though guided by developmentally appropriate practices and the NAEYC accreditation system, are hardly ideologically ubiquitous. Third, the case for the importance of quality and the need to raise it significantly has escaped policy makers who have the power to allocate resources. Although these policy makers may acknowledge the laments voiced about quality and compensation, given their accountability as elected officials, they are anxious to make a dent, to gain a big wallop for their investments. Funding slots so that more children are served is far more politically appealing than simply enhancing quality.

Therefore, a focus on quality is essential to safeguarding the investments already being made in ECEC in the United States. In particular, changes need to be made in the way standards are promulgated, implemented, and enforced, moving the process from one that is essentially minimalist to one that imposes regulations on this field in a manner commensurate with other human services domains. Quality enhancement is needed in the compensation and training requirements for those working in the field. Progress is underway in this area, with several national organizations and several significant efforts at state levels to establish strategies that could be replicated.

Public Understanding and Public Advocacy

It is said that no nation solves a social problem until there is widespread understanding that the problem exists. To this end, advocates for early childhood education, increasingly becoming more sophisticated, are building media campaigns in their work. New research studies are often accompanied by foundation support to disseminate or publicize the findings. Major media campaigns regarding brain research and a series of reports from the National Academy of Sciences—*Preventing Reading Difficulties in Young Children* (Snow, Burns, & Griffin, 1998), *From Neurons to Neighborhoods: The Science of Early Childhood Development* (Shonkoff & Phillips, 2000) and *Eager to Learn: Educating Our Preschoolers* (Bowman et al., 2001)—are noteworthy examples. Well recognized by the field and by foundation funders, these efforts will need to be expanded considerably, with the precise goal of ensuring that the American public (along with policy makers) are fully aware of the quality crises in ECEC. National organizations will need to create systematic strategies to mobilize their members, and training institutions will need to train future early childhood educators and caregivers to become involved in public engagement activities.

Governance and Finance

Despite considerable public and private investment in ECEC in the United States, there is no coordinated approach to governance; programs still compete for dollars, planning is done by programs, and financing is handled reactively rather than proactively. There is no sense of the whole—fragmentation, competition, and inefficiency are hallmarks of service provision. Given the episodic history of ECEC in the United States, these conditions are not surprising. Increasingly, those who see the field as a system rather than as individual programs understand and are advocating a need for some governance and funding mechanism that will allow early care and education to be seamed together so that parents and the public are not so confused about the field's intents and mechanisms. To date, there is no governance mechanism or public understanding of the need for one; this paucity relates directly to issues of public funding. Several states, however, recognizing the depth of the issues, have taken leadership to create ECEC systems (see Chapters 5 and 8). These can be models for other states that will need to cope with this problem in the next decade or face the collapse of ECEC.

Pedagogy and Programs

Appropriately, the United States has been focusing of late on policy issues in ECEC. However, serious pedagogical issues persist. Given changes in the U.S. population, advances in technology, and increasing demands being placed on young children for increased academic performance (see Chapter 6), pedagogical attention is warranted. In particular, with more women coming into the work force (see Chapter 1) as a result of welfare policies and income needs, an unprecedented number of infants and toddlers need early childhood services. Presently, the field does not have the capacity to handle this population in terms of adequate space, pedagogy, staff, and knowledge. Another social reality, an increasing incidence of violence, demands that early education programs address the issue from both security and pedagogical perspectives. Moving from societal to technological changes, ECEC will need to catch up to the effective use of technology for pedagogical, assessment, and management purposes. Assessment will continue to be a major issue, as policy makers press for greater accountability to justify early childhood program expenditures. Determining how to best assess young children and how to manage the information so that it is not used to harm children will be next-decade issues. The field will also need to come to grips with what it wants children to know and be able to do before any effective assessment system can be mounted.

Access

Though great strides to increase service access have been made, low-income children, those most likely to benefit from high-quality programs, are still underserved in comparison to their age counterparts from families who can afford to purchase quality services or services at all (see Chapter 3). Increasing access to services for all children is a policy imperative that will demand attention in the future. Moreover, given equity issues and population trends, there will be increasing urgency to create programs and services that address the needs of children from families whose dominant language is not English. Services for children with disabilities have received considered attention in the United States; still more needs to be done to address these children's specific needs, especially as such measures relate to the inclusion of these children in programs for typically developing children.

Energy and Invention

As noted previously, the 1990s witnessed a renaissance of ECEC in the United States. The federal government took the lead by establishing the Child Care Bureau within the U.S. Department of Health and Human Services and by funding the Early Childhood Institute within the U.S. Department of Education. The federal government has also supported many new research efforts. In addition, at the national level, numerous nongovernmental professional organizations have emerged and are doing exemplary work; those organizations with long histories have expanded their membership and roles considerably. At the state and local levels, scores of examples of innovation exist.

Yet, for this accomplishment, a serious front-line problem persists. For decades, U.S. early educators have worked for low wages, few benefits, and little job security. They have given their all to young children and to the field; indeed, people from other fields marvel, wondering constantly, "How do they do it?" With scores of opportunities for women and with monetary incentives that far surpass those offered by ECEC, attracting and retaining staff is increasingly difficult. Those who enter the ECEC work force are often demoralized quickly.

The single greatest challenge the field faces is to generate energy, fiscal resources, and enthusiasm to address the challenges outlined in this chapter. In part, this can be accomplished by creating new, badly needed incentives (salaries, compensation packages, professional development opportunities) and fellowship opportunities (see Chapter 5). In addition, however, the field will need some significant new boosts of energy. Although the field has been working diligently to create new standards and new programs, past policy advances have come largely from outside the field. Policy incentives have come from diverse sources—new and well-popularized research, attention from prestigious national organizations (e.g., the National Governors Association; the National Education Goals Panel, see Chapter 10), and investments by foundations which have created an early childhood funders' collaborative and supported many innovative efforts. Until there is a full-fledged, coordinated governmental policy, work will need to be done to sustain the commitment of those outside the ECEC field. These people outside of the field will need to invent, to question the field, and to make investments that are of systemic rather than programmatic orientation. Investments in research will need to continue, and the growing federal role in research will need to be sustained.

PROGNOSIS: CAN AND WILL THESE CHANGES HAPPEN?

The United States makes things happen incrementally, except when there is a threat of crisis. Until the American people internalize that young children are in jeopardy, action will remain incremental. The nation will continue to make policy by example. The issue of the rights of children, so prominent in other nations, does exist. The United States needs to do right by its children, but until the nation acknowledges the rights of children, it will move slowly. That the United States has not ratified the United Nations Convention on the Rights of the Child should not escape notice. This nation, great and glorious, needs a policy push. Our hope is that this book will help move us in that direction.

REFERENCES

Azer, S., LeMoine, S., Morgan, G., Clifford, R.M., & Crawford, G.M. (2002, Winter). Briefs: Regulation of child care. *Early Childhood Research and Policy Briefs, 2*(1). Chapel Hill: University of North Carolina at Chapel Hill, National Center for Early Development & Learning. Retrieved August 7, 2002, from http://www.fpg.unc.edu/~ncedl/PDFs/RegBrief.pdf

Bowman, B.T., Donovan, M.S., & Burns, M.S. (Eds.). (2001). *Eager to learn: Educating our preschoolers*. Washington, DC: National Academy Press.

Bredekamp, S. (1987). *Developmentally appropriate practice in early childhood programs serving children from birth through age 8*. Washington, DC: National Association for the Education of Young Children.

Bredekamp, S., & Copple, C. (Eds.). (1997). *Developmentally appropriate practice in early childhood programs* (Rev. ed.). Washington, DC: National Association for the Education of Young Children.

Clifford, R.M., Early, D.M., & Hills, T.W. (1999). Almost a million children in school before kindergarten: Who is responsible for early childhood services? *Young Children, 54*(5), 48–51.

Derman-Sparks, L., & the ABC Task Force. (1989). *Anti-bias curriculum: Tools for empowering young children*. Washington, DC: National Association for the Education of Young Children.

Elementary and Secondary Education Act of 1965, PL 89-10, 20 U.S.C. §§ 241 *et seq.*

Family and Medical Leave Act (FMLA) of 1993, PL 103-3, 5 U.S.C. §§ 6381 *et seq.*, 29 U.S.C. §§ 2601 *et seq.*

Kagan, S.L., & Cohen, N.E. (1997). *Not by chance: Creating an early care and education system for America's children. Abridged report. The Quality 2000 Initiative*. New Haven, CT: Yale University, Bush Center in Child Development and Social Policy.

National Association for the Education of Young Children (NAEYC). (1985). *Guide to accreditation by the National Academy of Early Childhood Programs*. Washington, DC: Author.

National Association for the Education of Young Children (NAEYC). (1991). *Guide to accreditation by the National Association for the Education of Young Children* (Rev. ed.). Washington, DC: Author.

National Association for the Education of Young Children (NAEYC). (1998). *Guide to accreditation by the National Association for the Education of Young Children: 1998 edition*. Washington, DC: Author.

Personal Responsibility and Work Opportunity Reconciliation Act of 1996, PL 104-193, 42 U.S.C. §§ 211 *et seq.*

Saluja, G., Early, D.M., & Clifford, R.M. (2001, Spring). Demographic characteristics of early childhood teachers and structural elements of early care and education in the United States. *Early Childhood Research and Practice, 4*(1). Retrieved August 7, 2002, from http://ecrp.uiuc.edu/v4n1/saluja.html

Schulman, K., Blank, H., & Ewen, D. (1999). *Seeds of success: State prekindergarten initiatives, 1998–1999*. Washington, DC: Children's Defense Fund.

Shonkoff, J.P., & Phillips, D.A. (Eds.). (2000). *From neurons to neighborhoods: The science of early childhood development.* Washington, DC: National Academy Press.

Snow, C.E., Burns, M.S., & Griffin, P. (Eds.). (1998). *Preventing reading difficulties in young children.* Washington, DC: National Academy Press.

Index

Page numbers followed by *f* indicate figures;
those followed by *t* indicate tables.

211